Spoon Fishing
for
Steelhead

Bill Herzog

Frank Amato Publications
P.O. Box 82112 • Portland, Oregon 97282
(503) 653-8108 • FAX: (503) 653-2766

Dedication

To my uncle, Robert Pollen, the best fisherman I've ever known. Without his patience and tutoring in my younger years, I would have never become a steelheader.

Acknowledgements

My thanks go out to everyone that selflessly gave their time and efforts to help me with this book: Jed Davis, for all his guidance, insights, and support; to Bradley Brian Bailey for his masterful slide photographs and for technical support in the preparation of this manuscript; to Hobart Manns for his information on spoon fishing history; to Philip Jensen and Ron Kovich for their hospitality; to the Gang; to Michael Cronen, the best friend and fishing partner a man could ask for; and especially my deepest thanks go to Frank and Nick Amato for giving me this wonderful opportunity.

Dreams do come true.

Copyright 1993 • Bill Herzog
Front Cover Photo: Brad Bailey
Book Design: Joyce Herbst • Typesetting: Charlie Clifford
Frank Amato Publications
P.O. Box 82112, Portland, Oregon 97282
(503) 653-8108 FAX: (503) 653-2766
Printed in Hong Kong
ISBN: 1-878175-30-0
UPC: 0-66066-00119-1

Contents

Introduction

Spoon fishing for steelhead is an in-depth, specialized technique. It is also one of the three oldest methods for hooking steelhead in rivers. But for far too long, spoons were treated as not much more than an afterthought by outdoor writers. What you've read has always been, "if technique A, B, or C does not produce, try running a spoon through the hole." Occasionally, spoons get a whole paragraph, perhaps two. There are many books and thousands of articles devoted to gear fishing for steelhead, yet spoons have received very little ink – until now. Their time has come!

This book is the result of 16 years of researching spoon techniques in the Northwest and British Columbia. But it's by no means just one man's findings or opinions. I look at it like a big puzzle – each piece representing a different person and their contributions to the big picture. The following pages are a product of journal notes that have been transfered into text. What you will read in the following chapters is all I know about spoon fishing for steelhead.

Of all the methods I enjoy using when pursuing steelhead (I dare you to name one that isn't enjoyable), drifting spoons is my number one love. Perhaps it is because I hooked my very first steelhead on a spoon, under the tutoring of my late uncle. Perhaps it is due to the dynamic strikes spoons evoke from steelhead. Or could it be that no other lure has provided me with such a treasure of river memories. I do know it is for those reasons I chose to research old and develop new spoon fishing techniques.

As tempting as they are to write about, I have stayed away from anecdotes. Fishing tales are fun to read, but rarely do you learn anything from them. As much as I love to re-create past battles with steelhead, my main objective here is to concentrate on information. Information you can use to spin your own fishing yarns.

This is not the "complete" book of spoon fishing for steelhead. I can't call it that because there are some areas, informational and geographical, not covered. One, this book was written from a West Coast perspective, specifically Washington, Oregon, and British Columbia. I have never fished in California, Idaho, or the Great Lakes tributaries with spoons. Not that I don't want to; I daydream often of fishing these rivers and hope to in the future. I cannot see writing about anything I have not researched and experienced firsthand. It would be unfair to the reader. However, steelheaders from these "un-researched" areas can take comfort in the fact that steelhead are steelhead, wherever they are found, and all react to a spoon the same way under given river conditions. With that in mind, I guarantee you can use the following information to hook steelhead anywhere on the planet that the sea-run rainbow dwells.

Throughout the pages of this book you will see many pictures of steelhead. They all have a few things in common. One, every single fish you see was released alive. Practicing catch and release will insure a future of steelhead runs in our rivers. Two, each fish was hooked during the 1990-91 season, the worst year for returns on the West Coast to date as of this writing. This should prove that persistence can and will pay off for you, even when chances for success are marginal. Many of the steelhead shown were caught on rivers that local "experts" had deemed were "dead" and not worth fishing.

I not only wanted to discuss spoon techniques, seasons, proper spoon choices and gear, but also some topics that never seem to appear with enough frequency in "how-to" books. This includes a short history of spoon fishing in relation to steelheading, an explanation of hydrodynamics, when to use spoons over other methods, and probably the most important aspect of any steelheading technique – how to become a respected as well as a successful steelheader. Oh, yes, I have saved the reader a bout with cliche' induced nausea by not using the phrase "spoon-fed" once.

I hope that no one expects me to reveal a quick, easy formula for hooking steelhead with spoons. I don't have any, and neither does anyone else. The content of this text is just a starting point, a compass of sorts to steer you in the right direction. The key to success is putting time in on the river; that fact is emphasized repeatedly in the following chapters. My magical success formula takes many years to mature, slow brewed by the fire of persistence. You have to put a lot of coins in the machine to hit the jackpot, so to speak.

The contents of this book will give the steelheader, beginner or seasoned veteran, a unique opportunity to peek at one of the many specialized techniques for doing battle with Pacific steelhead. It will also open some eyes by exposing old, accepted myths that surround steelheading, and spoon angling techniques. Finally, I think you will enjoy the many photos taken from all over the steelhead's range. They tell their own stories.

Welcome to spoon fishing for the greatest game fish in the world – my world.

– **Bill Herzog**
Tacoma, Washington

Chapter 1

Steelhead Spoons

Webster's Dictionary defines spoon as follows: "1. An eating or cooking implement consisting of a small shallow bowl with a handle. 2. Something that resembles a spoon in shape, usually a metal or shell fishing lure." It looks like Webster had his priorities in the wrong order. Fishermen that are familiar with the spoon's effectiveness as a steelhead attractor would define them as "a tool used to engage battle with America's premier game fish."

It's only fitting that America's greatest fish be angled for with a lure that is exclusively American in origin and development. The spoon is used by fishermen wherever steelhead are found – from British Columbia to the Great Lakes, and to an extent, South America and the Soviet Union. For thousands of North Americans who spoon

fish for steelhead, theirs is the only technique that employs a lure with such powerful action. The spoon's animation as it ambles through a drift seems to heighten awareness on the river. Spoons are as attractive as a technique to the steelheader as they are to his quarry.

This first chapter is for your information and entertainment. Before we dive headfirst into techniques, seasons, equipment, etc., I thought a look at some history, a clarification of hydrodynamics (what makes a spoon work) and a listing of commercially available spoons would be appropriate and enlightening. It will enrich your background on spoons, and give you a better understanding about the flashing bits of metal *Onchorhynchus mykiss* finds irresistible.

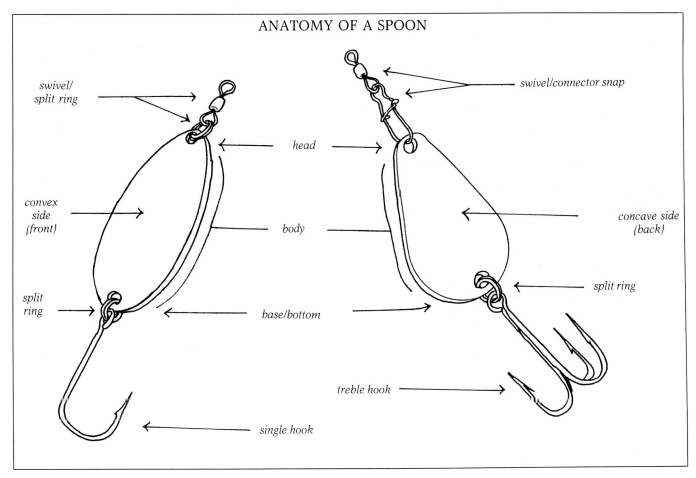

ANATOMY OF A SPOON

swivel/split ring

swivel/connector snap

head

convex side (front)

concave side (back)

body

split ring

split ring

base/bottom

treble hook

single hook

Spoon History 101:
The Inventor, The Innovator, and The Steelhead Pioneer

The history of spoon fishing is one rich in American flavor. Spoons are exclusively an American invention. Every early inventor and manufacturer came from within the states. Today, spoons are manufactured all over the world – even the Soviet Union produces a line of spoons. Spoons and their history have a long, storied background. To expound fully on the complete spoon biography would require an additional book. I would have writer's cramp, and you would probably be asleep before too long. So, for the sake of brevity and not losing the reader in an avalanche of unnecessary historical information, I've tried to keep this part of the chapter as short, yet informative, as possible.

Since the beginnings of spoon fishing in the early 1800s, many men have laid an indelible mark on their place in sport fishing history. Johnson, Lobb, Huntley, Hendryx, Shoff, Hofscneider, they all had a heavy hand in transforming spoon manufacturing from garage projects to big business.

There are, however, three men that stand head and shoulders above the rest. They have had the greatest effect on spoon fishing as we know it today; no one in the future is likely to top their achievements. This trio of revolutionaries is spotlighted here for their total contributions to spoon development, and the direct effect their work has had on steelhead fishing.

The Inventor

Every time an angler hooks a steelhead on a spoon, he should give thanks to a man born in 1806 in Vermont. Julio Thompson Buel is to spoon fishing what Henry Ford was to the auto industry. Many tales have been told by generations of sportsmen all over the country about how Julio Buel invented the spoon.

The Inventor, the man that started metal lure/spoon fishing. Julio Thompson Buel, "The Baitmaker Of Whitehall."

Buel made his discovery at the tender age of 15, in 1821. He loved to trout fish, and one of his favorite haunts was Lake Bomoseen (where it all began), seven miles north of his home in Castleton, Vermont. His target species back then was lake trout, and he trolled for them with worms and minnows whenever he had the chance.

It was a fall morning, the exact date lost in time, that the spoon's effectiveness on salmonids was first realized. In his book *The Spooners* author Harvey Thompson recalls, through museum records, the series of events that accidentally dropped Julio Buel into the lap of sport-fishing immortality.

"Here is the story Julio T. Buel told his (Whitehall, N.Y.) friends. He'd finished his bread and meat, washed it down with some cold, clean Lake Bomoseen water, and was enjoying some fruit out of an earthen jar. Suddenly, his drifting boat scraped against a submerged rock. Only a slight lurch, but sufficient enough to startle Julio and cause him to drop his spoon into the water. Over and over it twisted and turned, down into the depths. Before it disappear from view, a great trout lunged for it, grabbed it, and took off." The rest, at the risk of using another cliche', was history

One of the original Buel spoons, circa 1850.

When Julio returned home he pilfered another spoon from the pantry and went to work. He soldered a hook to the concave side, sawed off the handle and drilled a hole in the end (head). He soon returned to Lake Bomoseen and hooked two large lake trout, the first fish ever taken on a metal lure.

He eventually substituted his own metal dies to make spoons instead of converting the family cutlery. In 1827, Julio Buel took his "Buel Spoons" from Vermont to Whitehall, New York. Over the years, local outdoor writers caught wind of this amazing discovery, and subsequently an overwhelming demand for Buel Spoons resulted. This caused the need for the first spoon/fishing lure manufacturing company in America to be formed, the J.T. Buel Company of Whitehall, N.Y., established in 1848.

For almost 40 years all the backorders for the now famous spoons could not be filled. Julio Buel insisted that all spoons be made in the best hand-crafted ways, and that took time. The orders went on until his final days. If you ever visit New York State and want to see Buel's original spoon, it is on display in Whitehall in the Skenesborough Museum, (518) 499-0716. Julio Thompson Buel died in 1886, but his spirit will be with every spoon fisherman forever.

The Innovator

Even after Buel's death, his spoon and variations of it (mostly fluted-blade "spinner spoons") were a fisherman's main tool for 20 more years until Detroit working class man Lou Eppinger revealed his innovative spoon. Fishing reels in the early 1900s were, at best, crude mechanical instruments. Combine these with the heavy silk braided lines that soaked up water like a sponge, and you had one difficult set-up to cast with. Backlashes with these outfits were the norm. Lou Eppinger realized the answer to backlashes would be to develop a lure that would cut through the air on a cast, and also have action. As anyone that uses a level-wind reel today knows, the heavier the lure, the easier line pays off the spool on a cast. By 1912, Lou developed a spoon that weighed two ounces—plenty of weight to cast effectively.

Eppinger not only had a lure that was easy to cast, but it also had great action. The spoon was pounded out so it was thinner in the middle than on the edges. Buel's and earlier spoons were all uniform in thickness. It took Lou years to perfect his spoon. He was unaware of hydrodynamics, so he worked from the cuff. He hammered it, bent it here and there, tried three different metals—a long, arduous task. By the end of 1912, Lou Eppinger was ready to sell the first "classic" style spoon copied so extensively for over 80 years. The spoon was called the Osprey, named after the best "fisherman" Lou ever saw.

Lou Eppinger was the innovator of the first casting/spinning lure, a classic style spoon called the "Osprey." He later changed the name to the more well-known "Dardevle" in honor of the returning WWI Allies.

Unlike earlier round or slightly oval models, Eppinger's spoon was narrower, longer, heavier and had an offset curviture, which gave it unique action. It could be cast with accuracy into the wind, and most importantly, it caught fish. They worked so well that local sportsmen started a loyal following for them.

In 1918, at the end of World War 1, Lou Eppinger changed the name of the Osprey. He re-named the spoon the Dardevle, in honor of the returning U.S. Marines that were named the "Dare Devils" by the Allies. "Dardevle" was spelled as such because he thought religious individuals might find the word "devil" unappropriate. The years following saw a steady increase in sales.

During World War II all brass was snatched up by the government to make ammunition. This left lure manufacturers with steel as the only practical substitute. Replacing brass with steel and cheap metals was a terrible compromise; the lures would not hold their shape.

7

After WW II, the invention of the spinning reel and monofilament line (along with a steady supply of brass) produced a sportfishing explosion, with Lou Eppinger's Dardevles in the drivers seat. In the 1950s, Lou's nephew, Ed Eppinger, became president of a rapidly expanding company. Ed is still president of Eppinger Manufacturing as of this writing, and the Dardevle is still going strong, with sales topping three million annually.

The unmistakable head-shot of Lucifer with the trademark barber-pole red and white stripes. The classic one-ounce Eppinger Dardevle, along with being one the most popular spoons ever, was widely used for steelhead during the 1950's on all legendary Puget Sound streams.

The Dardevle was readily accepted as a steelhead spoon here in the Northwest. The one-ounce, red/white Dardevle was my uncle's favorite lure. Its magic worked for years during the glory days on Washington's Puyallup River in the 1950s. The red/white Dardevle was the hottest lure going, according to my uncle. He and his band of hotshot spoon fishermen threw Dardevles exclusively on the Puyallup, back when that river was the top steelhead producer in Washington State.

The Steelhead Pioneer

Julio Buel invented it, Lou Eppinger improved it, and C.V. Clark put it all together for the steelheader. C.V. Clark started Seneca Tackle Company in 1924 in Providence, Rhode Island. He realized that with the newfound popularity of the spinning reel, there were no spoons that were suitable for use as a spinning lure.

Clark designed the Wob-L-Rite—a fat teardrop style spoon that was small, compact, easy to cast, and had great action. When he introduced the lure on a trip to Oregon in 1930, local fishermen discovered the Wob-L-Rite's effectiveness on steelhead. So, as far as history is concerned, the Wob-L-Rite was the first steelhead spoon. This attracted a lot of attention to the Wob-L-Rite. Sales soon spread like wildfire all over the Northwest—first over Oregon, then up into Washington and Idaho— wherever steelhead were found.

In 1950, C.V. Clark also designed one of the most popular and widely copied spoons of today, the Little Cleo. The spoon's seductive wiggle reminded Clark of a famous belly dancer of the time named Cleo, henceforth the name. "Cleos" first gained popularity in the Great Lakes region. Castability, incredible action in river situations, word of mouth and advertising also made the Cleo one of the top steelhead spoons in the Northwest and British Columbia. The Wob-L-Rite and the Little Cleo are, along with the Dardevle, probably the most copied spoons of all time. C.V. Clark's company, now known as Acme Tackle Company, sells more Little Cleos than all their other lures combined.

With Clark's introduction of spoons to Northwest steelheaders, it gave fishermen in the 1930s an opportunity to catch their favorite fish on something new. Before the introduction of the Wob-L-Rite, only fly fishing and drifting roe were available techniques. Spoon fishing is one of the oldest methods for hooking steelhead in rivers, yet over the last 75 years was never developed to the extent of fly fishing and drift gear fishing. Why not is anyone's guess.

C.V. Clark was the first man to introduce a spoon especially for Northwest steelhead fishermen on a trip to Oregon in 1930. Even though fisheries and wildlife departments in British Columbia and Washington State have reported steelhead taken on "Spoon baits" as early as 1898, Clark's fat/teardrop Wob-L-Rite was the first documented steelhead spoon.

A few more curious points to ponder. Since the early 1950s, spoon manufacturers have not come up with any new spoon designs, just adaptations from existing products. The reason for this, believe it or not, is all spoon design possibilities have been explored. Therefore, what spoon designs you see in today's market (except for some "gimmick" designs that have no practical use on a steelhead river) will be the same ones, in all styles, you will see in the future. Another interesting note is that Eppinger Manufacturing still carries the Buel name in their catalog. J.T. Buel's original fluted blade spoon baits (actually large spinners) are exactly reproduced today, save for minor component improvements, the same way they looked back in 1850.

Julio Buel, Lou Eppinger, C.V. Clark – The Inventor, the Innovator, and the Steelhead Pioneer. They were the first ones to fill a great need by sportfishermen, and they personify the old adage of necessity being the mother of invention.

Pflueger heart-shaped "spoon blade" lure, circa 1890. Actually large spinners and not spoons at all, these lures were the first spinners ever in production.

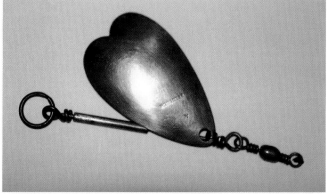

The Pearl Wobbler, circa 1920. All spoon companies of the era had a product made from mother of pearl, yet no manufacturer had the ability to make them in-house. Every spoon company ordered bodies from the same button maker in New York.

The Swing Wing, developed in the Northwest in the 1940's. One of the more unusual "gimmick"spoons of the time, it featured adjustable wings that would enhance or slow down its action.

By far the strangest spoon you will ever see. This is the Southbend Sunspot Spoon, made from 1910 to 1940. It featured a celluloid center, which made it translucent. The idea behind this gimmick was to give the illusion of a fish skeleton.

How Does A Spoon Work?

When a steelheader buys a certain style spoon, the influencial factors are usually price and "I heard it works on 'em." Purchasing spoons on heresay or from the bargain table will do you little good when faced with changing river conditions. Buying spoons blindly like this is similar to getting a new wardrobe without checking garment sizes. The chances of a match in either situation is slim. A good steelheader needs to know how each spoon design will perform and must eliminate guesswork when buying spoons. The first step is to understand how each style of spoon works. To help do that we have to discuss hydrodynamics, the science that deals with the motion of water.

Let's start with waves. All waves are the same, only the carrier differs. For example, we have radio waves, sound waves, ocean waves, etc. Two main factors determine the quality of a wave. These factors are "frequency" and "amplitude." Amplitude, or volume, is the power of the wave. Frequency determines how often the wave occurs. Using an ocean wave as an example, a one-foot wave has low power or amplitude, whereas a five-foot wave has greater power or amplitude. If a wave crashes into the shore every 30 seconds, this may be interpreted as a low frequency. But if conditions are such that a wave crashes onto shore every five seconds, this is a high frequency.

A fishing spoon is a wave that has been formed in metal. When it is moved through a medium such as air or (in this case) water, it acts like any other wave. And, like any other wave, it also has amplitude and frequency.

The two drawings show different amplitudes. In figure "A," the bottom hump, or wave, in the base of the spoon body is more pronounced. It has more power. It therefore produces a larger wave. In figure "B," this same bottom hump or wave is less pronounced. It has less power, and produces a smaller wave.

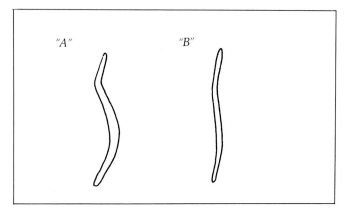

Although amplitude can be easily predicted by looking at the wave, frequency will be determined to a large extent by the speed it is pulled through the water. It will also be determined by the overall design of the spoon. In the figures alluded to a moment ago, we focused on the bottom hump, or wave, on the base of the spoon. Closer examination reveals that there are actually two waves in each lure. The top wave is much smaller than the bottom wave and is therefore less dominant in the overall action that will be imparted by the spoon. However, both waves are equally important because the amplitude and frequency (what we anglers refer to as "action") will be determined by the interaction of these two waves.

What is happening? How is movement or "action" created in the water? This is the toughest part to grasp, but if you come to understand the following, you will be able to look at any spoon, and without ever making a cast, be able to make a fairly educated guess as to how action will be imparted on the spoon when it is reeled through the water.

In figure "C," what you see is a silhouette of a very simple spoon body, one similar to Julio Buel's original invention. Let's call it the "SS" for "simple spoon." Note the path of the water as illustrated by the arrows.

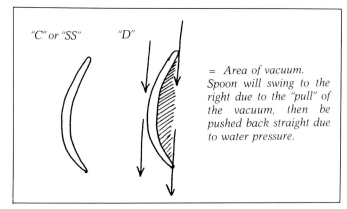

= Area of vacuum. Spoon will swing to the right due to the "pull" of the vacuum, then be pushed back straight due to water pressure.

Water is passing on both the left and the right of the SS at an equal rate. When this spoon is run through the water, the spoon will swing right and then straighten out. This same pattern will be repeated. Again, what is happening? Note in figure "D" that water pressure on both sides of the spoon is not equal. Water is running up against the left side fairly easily but because of the design, the right hand tip (as marked) on the head of the spoon is blocking water from running up the right side. As a result, water is running parallel to the concave area (marked). As a result, (1) A vacuum has been created in the concave area because it is receiving no water pressure; (2) Water running parallel to the concave area is creating suction. This vacuum and suction is the force that moves the blade to the right.

Before we move on, three points must be made. First, the spoon will be pushed back into a straight position. This is because when the concave portion is broadside to the current, the water pressure is too great and it gets pushed back into a straight position. Of course, once it goes back to the straight position, another vacuum is formed on the right side and the bottom hump on the base of the SS swings out. It's the back and forth motion that gives the spoon "action."

The second point is this: if we create a larger wave or hump, we will be creating a larger vacuum, greater pressure and more suction. This will result in a more severe movement of the SS.

The third point is this: each style of spoon has a speed threshold. The afformentioned dynamics only work within a given speed range for each particular spoon. If, for example, too much speed is applied to a Wob-Lure, it will abort its action and swim in a tight spiral, like a plug-cut herring. On the other hand, if you take a high speed salmon spoon like a Northport Nailer that is intended for downrigger fishing and troll it at 1.5 m.p.h., it will gently sway from side to side imparting little or no action.

How does this translate into spoon action? Spoon action can be regulated by the amplitude of the wave or bend in the metal. A spoon like the Krocodile has a strong wave or bend. On the other hand, a T.B.S. (thin-bladed spoon) has a very weak wave or bend. This is intentional. A strong wave is needed when you want to impart action at a slow speed. A weak wave is needed when when you want action at high speeds. In general, trolling spoons have a weak wave and are not practical for use in river steelheading situations. Shoff's Triple Teaser is a good example of this. The lure is virtually a flat piece of metal. Great for trolling for trout in lakes, but not much use to the steelheader. On the other hand, a Little Cleo or B.C. Steel cannot be fished with speed. These lures are at their best when cast and retrieved at a modest speed or drifted for steelhead in rivers.

As previously noted, most spoons have two waves. In most cases, one of these waves is much more dominant, but the second wave or bend gives added action in tandem with the first to create a rythmn or action which experimentation and experience proved to be appealing.

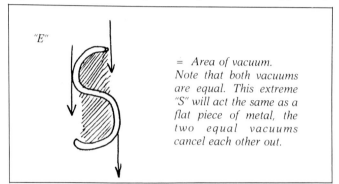

= Area of vacuum. Note that both vacuums are equal. This extreme "S" will act the same as a flat piece of metal, the two equal vacuums cancel each other out.

Figure "E" is interesting to note. What you see is a perfectly balanced "S" curve. See how both humps are very pronounced? You would think that on a spoon like this the action on the retrieve would be very animated. Not so! This spoon is perfectly balanced on both sides. Equal vacuums are being created. As a result, the spoon stays straight! This brings up an important point about spoons. It is the disparity in pressure that creates action. A piece of flat metal has no or very little action. It tracts true. But as soon as we change one of the humps on the "S" spoon, action will increase.

In figure "F," we see a typical spoon with two waves. The bottom wave is very pronounced, but the top one is

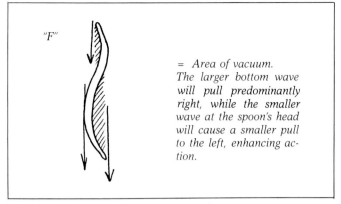

= Area of vacuum. The larger bottom wave will pull predominantly right, while the smaller wave at the spoon's head will cause a smaller pull to the left, enhancing action.

hardly noticeable. The bottom wave will pull left, but when pressure is equalized and it swings back straight, the top wave will give the spoon a slight action to the right – thus action is enhanced.

Finally, we must consider the width of the spoon blade. A wider blade encompasses more surface area. It will therefore create, relative to a narrower blade, more vacuum and more pressure. A simple rule of thumb can be applied to spoons: a narrower spoon will create less action relative to a wider spoon of the exact same configuration. High speed trolling spoons or T.B.S. tend to be narrower than casting spoons like the Dardevle, Koho, or Wob-L-Rite.

A final point can be made regarding the relationship of amplitude to frequency. The full potential of amplitude can only be realized within a certain frequency range. If the spoon is worked too slowly, there will be no amplitude or "action". We see this on high speed trolling spoons. Conversely, a B.C. Steel or a Stee-Lee can only stand so much speed. At too low a speed, amplitude diminishes and action is lost.

This part of the chapter should give you an insight on spoon dynamics. Now you will be able to go to the tackle shop and make a fairly accurate judgement of how each style of spoon will react in different river situations before you buy them.

Spoon Styles And Commercial Brands

Take a trip down to any major retail fishing tackle outlet and check out the pegboard spoon display. To the casual observer it would seem that the choices of color, design, finish, and weight are endless, not to mention confusing. The question inevitably arises, "do I need all these different styles of spoons to catch steelhead?" The answer is no! Many spoons on today's market are nothing more than gimmicks and/or badly reproduced imitations of popular styles.

It's an unfortunate fact of manufacturing – some companies cut corners in production to deliver a less expensive facsimile of a popular design. But, as with any item and not just spoons, when quality is compromised, inferiority is the standard result. All the commercially available spoons that are listed here are proven designs that have performed the best in steelhead rivers over the years. Not just in fish attracting qualities, but also responsiveness, action, quality finishes, and availability.

All listed are stamped out of high quality brass. Brass holds its shape indefinitely, unlike cheaper, softer metals.

Any brand name that has been omitted from the list fell into one of the four rejection catagories: (1) Ineffectual design; (2) poor quality metals; (3) impractical for river use, or; (4) unavailable in wide market. A number of very popular brand name spoons are left out here because they are designed primarily for Great Lakes/saltwater salmon trolling, or open water jigging. In either case, these spoon designs do not adapt well to river fishing situations.

All the commercially available practical designs can be broken down into four catagories: (1) the fat teardrop, (2) the oval, (3) the classic, and (4) the elongated. These four, including one style of T.B.S. used for plunking, are the styles of spoons that will cover all holding water situations you will encounter on the river. They are the only styles of spoons that respond and function adequately to meet the river steelheader's standard of demands.

These spoon styles and brand names are not exclusive choices of the author. Untold numbers of steelheaders voted in this "election," from famous guides to old timers, greenhorns, friends and many on the river acquaintances. This part of the chapter is one more "section of the puzzle."

Style: Fat Teardrop
Description: Tall triangular in shape, typically narrow head, tapered open to the widest area of the body on the base.
Weights: 1/4, 1/2, 5/8th ounce.
Most Effective: In shallow runs, 1-1/2 to 4 feet deep, or very slow, almost slack water, performs best in tailout/riffle situations.

Fat/Teardrop

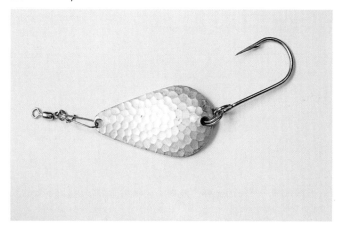

Brand Names/Manufacturers:
Wob-Lure – Wordens/Yakima Bait Co.
Stee-Lee – Acme Tackle Co.
Wob-L-Rite – Acme Tackle Co.
Kit-A-Mat – Gibbs/Nortac Co.
KO Wobbler – Acme Tackle Co.

Style: Oval
Description: Narrow head, gradually widens to middle of the body, (the widest area) tapering downward to a narrow base, "football" shaped.
Weights: 1/2, 2/5, 2/3, 3/4, 5/8, 1 ounce.
Most Effective: Moderate to fast flow, four to ten feet deep, best at the ends of riffle breaks to mid-pool.

Oval

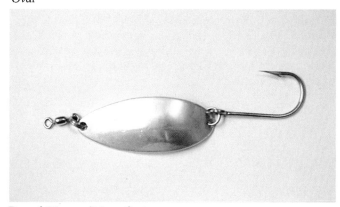

Brand Names/Manufacturers:
Little Cleo – Acme Tackle Co.
B.C. Steel – Pen Tac Inc.
Koho – Gibbs/Nortac Co.
Devle Dog – Eppinger Mfg. Co.
Krocodile Stubby – Luhr Jensen Co.
Johnson Silver Minnow (Sprite) – Johnson Co.

Style: Classic
Description: Narrow to small head, tapers open gradually to the widest point at the base.
Weights: 1/2, 2/5, 2/3, 3/4, 1 ounce.
Most Effective: Mid-pool drifts, moderate to fast flow, 4 to 12 feet deep.

Classic

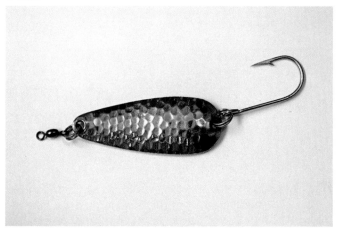

Brand Names/Manufacturers:
Dardevle – Eppinger Mfg. Co.
Wonder Lure – Yakima Bait Co.
Pixee – Blue Fox Tackle Co.
Pro Lure – Luhr Jensen Co.
Tony Acetta's Spoon – Luhr Jensen Co.

12

Style: Elongated

Description: Very narrow head, long, slim body tapering out slightly to widest spot 3/4 of the way down the body, tapers slightly to base. Extreme foil (curvature).

Weights: 1/2, 3/4, 1 ounce.

Most Effective: Very deep and/or fast water, fastest sinking spoon, best when jigged or worked vertically at slow speeds.

Elongated

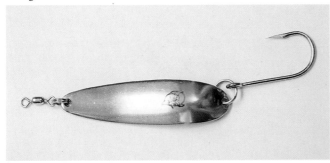

Brand Names/Manufacturers:
Krocodile – Luhr Jensen Co.
Syclops – Mepps (Sheldons, Inc.)
Cop-E-Cat – Eppinger Mfg. Co.

Style: Thin Blade (Plunking)

Description: Diamond-shaped, widest spot in middle of spoon body. Extremely thin profile.

Weights: 1/8, 3/16th ounce. No. 1 and 2 sizes, respectively.

Most Effective: When "plunked" in current edges. (See Chapter 3, "Plunking the Thin-Bladed Spoon")

Thin-Blade

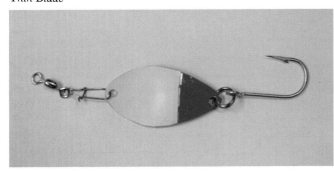

Brand Names/Manufacturers:
F.S.T. – Shoffs, Inc.

Here is a listing of manufacturers/mail order houses where you can send for spoons or information on their availability:

Shoffs, Inc. (F.S.T's, Triple Teasers)
P.O. Box 231
Kent, Washington 98032
(206)-852-4130

Eppinger Manufacturing Co. (Dardevles, Devle Dogs, Cop-E-Cats)
6340 Schaefer Highway
Dearborn, Michigan 48126
(313)-582-3205

Luhr Jensen and Sons, Inc. (Krocodile, Krocodile Stubby, Pro Lure, Tony Acetta's Spoon)
P.O. Box 297 – 400 Portway
Hood River, Oregon 97031
(503)-386-3811

Wordens' Lures/Yakima Bait Co. (Wob-Lure, Wonder Lure)
P.O. Box 310
Granger, Washington 98932-0310
1-800-252-4888

Pen Tac Corporation (B.C. Steel)
P.O. Box 18273
Seattle, Washington 98118

Blue Fox Tackle (Pixee)
645 North Emerson
Cambridge, Minnesota 55008

Acme Tackle, Inc. (Little Cleo, Wob-L-Rite, KO Wobbler, Stee-Lee)
69 Bucklin Street
Providence, Rhode Island 02907

Gibbs/Nortac Co. (Koho, Kit-A-Mat)
7455 Conway Avenue
Burnaby, British Columbia V5E-2P7

Mepps/Sheldons', Inc. (Syclops)
Dept. 174
Antiago, Wisconsin 54409-2496

Angling Specialties (Teardrop style spoon bodies, 4 finishes)
19520 McLoughlin Blvd.
Gladstone, Oregon 97027
1-503-650-1930

Bass Pro Shops (Dardevles, Little Cleos, Pixee, Syclops)
1935 South Campbell
Springfield, Missouri 65898-0123
1-800-227-7776

Cabela's (Little Cleos, Dardevles)
812 – 13th Avenue
Sidney, Nebraska 69160
1-800-237-4444

Fisherman's Shack (Classic and teardrop style spoons, 5 finishes)
9465 Airlie Rd.
Monmouth, OR 97361
1-800-292-6395, 1-503-838-6395

Chapter 2
Why Spoons Over
Other Methods?

Ask any steelheader, and he or she will tell you about their favorite method of hooking fish. Beginners or experts, everyone has a particular method they would prefer to fish with. If the steelheader is successful with a certain method, I'll be the first one to recommend they do not change to a different one.

For the majority of river fishermen the challenge of drifting bait, senses honed sharp for the delicate mouthing of the offering, is the only way to go. Some revel in the hard slamming strike on a well presented diving plug. For others, a spinner worked expertly through a shallow riffle provoking an attack from an enraged torpedo is the ultimate high. And possibly nothing in steelheading is as exciting as watching a summer run inhale a waking dry fly. Arguing which method is most gratifying is moot. Everyone is different.

Each technique has its plus factors that make it efficient for hooking steelhead. And to become a true expert with your chosen technique, you must learn to fish with it in all combinations of river conditions and situations. But the steelheader that restricts himself to one method year around will at times be handicapped by refusing to switch to a more efficient one. There will always be river conditions where one technique will out-fish another consistently. Let me give you some examples.

A fly fisherman, fishing only on the surface with waking flies is paired up with a drift fisherman armed with No. 6 fluorescent Spin-N-Glos and sand shrimp. Both are fishing on a 42 degree, high water winter river in January. Who would you put your money on? Because of very cold water temperatures, restricted visibility and strong flow, the bait fisherman working his drift bobber/bait combination slowly along the bottom in the current edge will clean house, while the fly guy trying to work the surface with a swift moving piece of fur is going to get nothing but casting practice. The steelhead could not see the fly, much less be excited enough to move to the surface to take it.

Now lets take the same two steelheaders and drop them on a 58 degree, low water summer river in August. Now who would you put the rent money on? Because of warmer water temperatures, clear, unrestricted visibility, ultra-high metabolism of fish, and gentle water flows, the dude tossing the Spin-N-Glo is going to send every fish in the drift fleeing in terror over this gaudy whirling

By nature, steelhead slam spoons. No subtle take that is common when drifting bait. These hard takes tell beginners they're in business.

knob. The fly guy, on the other hand, will experience explosive surface takes on his waking dry.

I realize these examples are extreme, but I wanted to make a clear point. Each steelheader would have greatly increased his chances for success by using the other's technique. The key is flexibility. There are too many otherwise good steelheaders that say, "I only fish eggs," or "I only pull plugs" – you get the picture. Not to say that fishermen that employ only one method are not successful; any method that is practiced and perfected will take a lot of steelhead in a lot of conditions, but not all conditions! Nor will spoons take steelhead under all conditions, but they will give you an added dimension under certain river circumstances.

Let's face it, there aren't as many steelhead around as there were when Eisenhower was in the Oval Office, so staying flexible for changing river conditions will make you a better steelheader. Just like the fly and Spin-N-Glo fishermen previously mentioned, under certain conditions spoons have a decisive advantage.

In this chapter we'll look at the advantages spoons give over other methods, how beginning steelheaders can use spoons to ease into their new sport, how veterans can uncomplicate days spent on the water, and even show how spoons will hook you up with trophy sized steelhead.

A Beginner's Best Friend

There is never a more awkward or impressionable time in the life of a stream fisherman than when the first step is made toward steelheading. First impressions are lasting ones. Many steelheaders have had experienced mentors, showing them the correct technique at the right time of year on the best section of a chosen river. Under these circumstances, which are usually favorable in all aspects, the newcomers will take their new sport to heart and make steelheading a part of their lives. On the flip side of the coin is the curious fisherman who wants to give steelheading a try, but has no one to teach him, no idea what river to start on, or what technique to start with. A greenhorn tackling a river blindly with mismatched drift gear is staring certain failure in the face, and interest is lost as quickly as his oft-snagged terminal tackle. A beginner can do himself a great deal of justice by starting off with spoons.

Before learning how to read holding water and how to choose the right spoon, the beginner must learn to cast accurately. Usually with the shift to steelheading is the change from spinning reels to level-wind reels. Those of you that use level-wind reels know the key to easy casting is to have plenty of weight on the terminal end–the more weight the easier line is payed off the spool on the cast. The result is increased distance and greater accuracy by not having to really whip the rod to cast. Therefore, there is less chance for a backlash. Terminal tackle is, 95 percent of the time, a greater degree lighter than a spoon used under the same conditions. The smaller, concentrated weight of the spoon casts easily for the beginner, and allows him to be familiarized with the new piece of equipment before trying to cast lighter terminal gear.

If you make the transition to steelheading and bring along your trusty spinning reel, that's fine. Some fishermen are not comfortable with level-wind reels.

A swivel, two split rings, and a hook. Spoons keep it simple for the beginner. One knot to tie on these uncomplicated lures, and all that's left to do is make a cast.

Large boulders like these can pose quite a problem when steelhead lay amongst them. As this fish found out, a spoon worked over the top of the tackle-eaters can coax them to come up and strike. Brad Bailey photo.

Anglers using spinning reels can also take advantage of the spoon's concentrated weight. Casts can be placed with much more accuracy. Unfortunately the spin fisherman loses some advantages to the level-wind fisherman.

The typical terminal drift gear setup is weighted in two spots, the lead or slinky on one end and drift bobber/bait/hook on the other. When casting, the two weights work against each other, pulling one another off-center, making casts land not quite where they were intended. A lot of you may say bushwah to that, knowing full well that you are extremely accurate with slinky and bait. Remember, we are talking to beginners here, and you probably have had much practice with this technique. The spoon, being one concentrated weight, travels in a slightly straighter path. The spoon has less air friction, giving longer flight for energy exerted in casting. Spoons do catch air to a degree, but are aerodynamically superior to cast than most forms of drift gear.

It is important that reaction time (for a beginner that really doesn't know what a steelhead bite feels like) is prolonged for that extra second. When drift fishing there will always be time between when a steelhead picks up the bait/drift bobber and when you actually feel it. After the fish picks it up, your lead must travel double the length of your leader before the line tightens and the "throb" of the bite is felt. Even if you only use a 16-inch leader, the lead must travel 32 inches before anything is noticed. A precious second or two is lost. An expert bait fisherman will be alert for that pause and be able to get a hook-set before the steelhead rejects his offering.

Beginners don't have the luxury of experience. When a steelhead halts a spoon's drift, it is felt immediately because everything stops simultaneously–line and lure. By the very nature of the way a steelhead usually slams a spoon, an instant hard yank is easier to detect than a delayed, subtle pick-up. Also, the "throb-throb-throb" of a working spoon is a hundred times easier for a neophyte to feel than the bounce of lead or slinky on the bottom.

Proper rigging of terminal gear can be confusing to a combinations of riggings to befuddle the poor newcomer. Spoons can eliminate the confusion. One simple knot is all the beginner must learn. If he or she already knows a strong, dependable knot, it only has to be tied once and you are fishing.
be tied once and you are fishing.

The beginner should find one weight and style of spoon to learn with. This is to familiarize themselves with the spoon's action and the proper depth and speed it should be fished—along with learning to cast it accurately. The less variables for the beginner, the easier it is for them to concentrate on fishing. I would suggest starting with a 1/2 ounce, brass or nickel finish spoon in the classic style to learn with. It covers the greatest amount of situations and conditions.

A half-dozen of these spoons in a small plastic box is all the newcomer needs for a day on the river. Learning to work water properly is enough to try and absorb without the confusion of putting together a 10-piece terminal package. Remember, ease of casting, greater distance with more accuracy, detecting the strike, and eliminating multiple knots and drift gear combinations are all reasons for the beginner to choose spoons.

Spoons = Simplicity

The last section discussed the multiple reasons for beginners to start off on the long road to steelhead success with the aid of spoons. One of the big factors was simplicity. It freed up the beginner from the bonds of complexity. The beginner, however, is not the only steelheader that can benefit from employing spoons. Veteran steelheaders can also take a leaf from the newcomer's book of simplicity. There are several good reasons for the experienced angler to choose spoons.

Simplicity with spoons carries weight in an area most give little thought to: river regulations. Years past have seen few or no special regulations on any steelhead river. This is not the case today. Many of the more popular rivers have gear restrictions, such as bait bans and artificial lure sections. British Columbia leads the way with these laws. The majority of the better rivers there are artificial lure only year around. Here in Washington, great rivers like the Skagit, Skykomish, and Sauk all have gear restrictions during the latter part of the winter steelhead season to protect the fragile, late native fish runs. I'm not familiar with individual river's seasonal restrictions in other states, but the artificial lure rule is certainly there. Here is where spoons help simplify your gear choice.

With spoons, as long as the river section is open for gear fishing, the addition of a single hook is all that's needed to be angling legally in any portion of the river. You have an effective lure to use anywhere in the river without having to carry extra gear. The addition of a single hook is done because of gear restrictions. Artificial lure sections/times of year are also governed by single hook restrictions. So you see, less money is spent for alternative gear for special sections of rivers and times of year. By using spoons, you are always legal to fish.

Have you ever wanted a day on the river that you didn't have to trip over several tackle boxes in your drift boat? Wouldn't a day of bank stomping be easier without 30 pounds of a stuffed to the seams vest draped over your shoulders? If you answered "no" to both questions, you probably enjoy complexity and a curved spine. Most steelheaders want or need a break once in a while. A box of six to a dozen varied style and color spoons, extra hooks and swivels, a hook file or sharpener, and a pair of pliers is all the veteran steelheader needs for an outing. This can all be carried in one pocket or pouch—no bulky vest to restrict movement. The whole outfit weighs perhaps two pounds. Compare that to packing 20—a day of walking the river will be completed with less fatigue. Plus you only have one knot to tie and you are fishing. Now isn't that simple?

All that is needed for a day's fishing on a steelhead river: a pair of cutter/pliers, a hook sharpener, and an assortment of designs, weights, and finishes to cover possible river conditions.

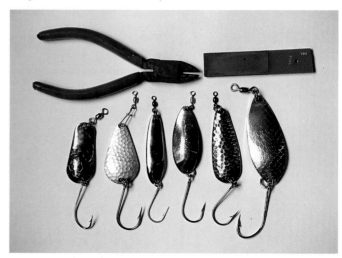

Time Is Precious

Steelheaders are always be ready to debate. Ask a hundred steelheaders what their favorite method of fishing is and you will likely receive a hundred different answers. There are two issues, however, that you will always get the same answers from everyone. One is the undying passion for steelhead and the rivers they live in. The other is the value of the time each steelheader gets to spend on the water. I know my most precious times are the hours I get to spend walking my favorite river on the Olympic Peninsula, and I want to make every second count. Spoons help me do just that.

First, let's look at what is considered to be the spoon's biggest advantage over most methods. The spoon, unlike flies or drift gear (manufactured up to this writing), gives off considerable flash. This flash is perceived at a greater distance by steelhead than flies or drift gear. Whereas a steelhead in normal visibility conditions (four to six feet) can see the spoon from four to five feet away, flies/drift gear, being subtle and smaller, can only be seen by steelhead at about half that distance.

This March native was hooked during an afternoon trip to a suburban river. Spoons gave the angler the opportunity to work twice as much water in the allotted few hours before dark to find this fish. Brad Bailey photo.

What this means is that it requires less casts to cover a fish holding area thoroughly with a spoon. The spoon's flash draws steelhead from greater distances than most methods—simple fact. Fewer casts needed to cover an area means less time spent working that piece of water.

That is how spoons save time. You can work two to three times the area that a fly/drift fisherman can in the same amount of time, and work it thoroughly.

To help illustrate my point, here is a hypothetical situation. You are bank fishing with drift gear. Each section of holding water is 30 feet long. Each cast takes approximately 1-1/2 minutes to complete. Since you want to work the water thoroughly, and drift gear is only effective in a two foot radius, it would take 15 casts and a little over 22 minutes to fish it completely. Now work the same water with spoons. Because of the greater area of attraction (four foot radius compared to two) and the fact that a spoon works slightly faster through the water than drift gear (about one minute per cast), it only requires seven or eight casts and less than ten minutes to cover the drift thoroughly.

When this formula is carried a bit further, you can see where a spoon fisherman can work three holes in less time than it takes a drift/fly fisherman to work two. And every inch of water is covered completely. If you only have an hour to fish a local river in the morning or after work, you can fish twice as much water in your allotted time, and that means twice the chance to hook a steelhead.

Do any other methods save time for the steelhead angler by attracting fish from a greater distance? Yes, spinners do, and to a degree, diving plugs. Spinners give off as much, if not more, flash than spoons, so their attraction quality is not questioned. The difference is spoons are fished in an alternate style, and on occasion, in much different holding water. (See Chapter 3 for details.) Plugs can also draw steelhead from a greater distance than drift/fly gear, but the type of water plugs are used in is generally restricted. Classic plug water on any river is few and far between, so all the water that would be passed up that could be fished with spoons is wasted—no time advantage here.

As I mentioned earlier, there aren't as many steelhead around as there were when the Pflueger Supreme was the reel on the cutting edge. Where there used to be dozens of fish in a section of river, today there may be only one. Today you need to employ a technique that gives you increased opportunities for a hookup. It just makes sense that the more water covered in a day the better the odds for success.

Over, Under, And In-Between

So far in this chapter many of the spoon's advantages have been discussed, but the question of its ability to fish water that some methods cannot has not yet been brought up. Spoons can allow you to fish water most steelhead fishermen cringe at.

Many times during a season you will encounter river

areas that always hold steelhead, but you see no one fishing here because they are serious tackle grabbers. You know the scenario— right in the middle of the "sweet spot" is a maze of tree limbs or unforgiving boulders that suck up every bit of gear sent down. Frustrating, but that's nature. So, just forget about the area completely, pass it up and fish elsewhere on the drift? No way! It can be fished, and fished so effectively with spoons you will be looking for places like this instead of avoiding them.

In his book, *Spinner Fishing For Steelhead, Salmon, and Trout,* spinner wizard Jed Davis discusses how, for the first and only time I am aware of, to utilizing the attracting qualities of the spinner to draw steelhead up from those "impossible" to fish snaggy spots. This presentation can be as much as three feet above the fish's lumber and boulder sanctuary. The same technique can be incorporated to spoon fishing. The spoon also gives off a great amount of flash. You may still donate a spoon or two to these nasty spots until you get the "feel" of how deep it can be worked over the snags.

Water like this is passed by most steelhead fisherman. Working a spoon through deep, choppy water can produce trophy steelhead.

After you get familiar with these spots over the course of the season, I guarantee they will not only produce steelhead for you on slim days, but will be a constant source of entertainment as well, especially if you frequent popular rivers. Entertaining? Here's a scenario I have had the pleasure of experiencing a few times.

If the author wasn't standing in the way, you would see two large trees slanting into the river next to the bank. This 17 lb. female was "lured" out from her sanctuary by the flash of a silver plated spoon.

Imagine having to share the river with one of those wonderful individuals that absolutely has to fish the water ahead of you all day. Nothing, and I mean nothing is more entertaining to me than watching grit-your-teeth-firstwater-or-die "sportsmen" pass up one of these "unfishable" spots. I can't help but laugh out loud while my partner or myself work a spoon behind them in these spots, because I know what is coming up next! The look on their faces when the steelhead jumps is priceless. You can hear their jaws dropping a mile away. I love giving these morons a taste of their own medicine. Chalk up another one for spoons.

Fishing over the top of these snaggy areas is not always possible. Sometimes there are so many branches on top of, in the middle of, and on the bottom of fish holding areas no technique can bring them out. These are true steelhead sanctuaries. In many cases, however, branches or trees are only in the top 2/3 of the drift. In other words, the surface and middle of the river flow is clogged, while the bottom remains clean. This situation calls for a technique that can draw steelhead out from under the obstruction.

To understand this situation, let's go back a bit to the spoon's ability to attract from greater distances. Whereas a cast with fly/drift gear would not be perceived by the fish, a spoon put in the same place will draw the steelhead out from under the trees to strike. In this situation the fish could see the spoon's flash whereas it could not see the terminal gear used in other techniques.

Another problem area you may encounter will be on small streams, but may also occur in isolated spots on larger rivers. You will invariably come upon a spot that is just big enough to hold one steelhead. These fish will be nudging their noses right up against the end of a log, small boulder, brush pile, clay ledge, etc. Because the fish has his head almost touching the obstruction, any attempt to drift bait by in the steelhead's range of vision would be impossible. No matter how short a leader is practical to use, by the time the lead has reached the fish, the bait has zipped over its head, unnoticed. As long as the bait and weight are separate, it is very difficult to reach these fish. A spoon is weight and lure in one, so when it reaches the face-buried steelhead, everything arrives at the same time. Spoons are a wonderful method to pull fish out from under these spots. (See Back-trolling The Spoon, Chapter 3.)

All of these spoons versus drift gear arguments may give you the impression that I don't favor drift gear fishing for steelhead – that I have a dislike for it. Not the case! I would estimate that 75 percent of my time on rivers is spent drift fishing with bait or drift bobbers. I'm in no way an exclusive spoon tosser. Spoons, like other methods of steelhead fishing, have their times and places on rivers when they almost can't be beat.

The Trophy Lure

Every steelheader, beginner or veteran, shares the same dream. Some talk about it more than others. Some consider it the motivating factor behind steelhead fishing. Others will try and tell you that it's just not important. But the dream is there, in every single steelheader alive today. If you are one of the lucky one in 100,000, you know what I'm talking about. The fish of a lifetime, a steelhead of 20 or more pounds. The true Holy Grail of the sport.

Every tackle manufacturer out there would like to think that they have "the lure" that consistently sorts out the big, trophy steelhead for the user. No one can make that exclusive claim, but there are some lures that definitely consistently appeal to huge steelhead. Spoons are lures that do just that, and they do it better than any other lure. In order to understand what makes the spoon a trophy lure, we have to look at the type of water trophy steelhead prefer.

The thrill and beauty of power. When giant steelhead like this one ambush your spoon, it is an experience to remember for a lifetime.

Over two decades of steelheading, I've been extremely fortunate to have brought 16 of these leviathans to hand, with 13 of them coming to the spoon. Lucky? Well, luck has a little to do with the fish being there, but that is where it stops. In regards to steelheading, luck is nothing more than preparation meeting opportunity. That in itself is the true essence of steelhead fishing. Over the years I've learned to recognize the style of water huge steelhead rest in. And it's not easy water to fish.

Trophy steelhead water will have three important ingredients. One is depth. They prefer the deepest possible steelhead holding water. These giants are not the average six to ten pound fish that can be comfortable in a few feet of broken water. Like a Chinook salmon, they need deeper water to hide their larger bodies from predators. You will never see, nor take, a 20-pound fish from any area less than six feet deep. So, no matter what river condition you are fishing in, concentrate on the deepest portion of the fishable steelhead holding water.

The second ingredient is a broken surface. This surface chop is caused by the third ingredient, large rocks and boulders. The hydraulics of water against the boulders is what creates the chop on the surface. What can be described as "chop" can be foot-high mini waves to one- to four-inch ripples on the surface. Big steelhead love turbulence. They will seek out river sections that have basketball sized or larger boulders in them. A trophy fish will lay behind and alongside the rocks that divert underwater current, requiring less effort to hold its mass in the flow. A broken or choppy surface tells you large boulders are present.

All the ingredients combined equal a recipe for trophy steelhead: deep, bouncy water with a boulder bottom. Now that you know what type of water to concentrate on, you need an effective technique to get down to them, and make the giants strike. Here is where spoons literally "shine."

19

A technique must be employed that can be presented easily in the deeper, heavy water, and will sufficiently excite them into striking. Because of their size and the amount of energy it requires to move themselves through the current, these behemoths are not going to leave their position unless something really gets them worked up. In order to show the spoon's effectiveness here, a look must first be made at other techniques in this type of water.

The fly fisherman can reach the fish with a Hi-D or fast sinking line like a Deep Water Express, but most flies, being relatively small and fast moving, would have to be put right in the fish's face—the steelhead would not be "excited" enough to move far for it. Diving plugs are a great exciter for big steelhead. However, positioning a drift boat in choppy, heavy water is tough, if not impossible. And, many rivers that are well known for their trophy sized steelhead do not allow fishing from a floating device. Not many spots on rivers are advantageous to work a plug from the bank, and as a rule, well-defined plug water on any river system is limited. Spinner fishermen will have some difficulty because most spinners that are weighted heavy enough to reach deep holding fish don't spin properly. A drift fisherman, armed with a heavy slinky and a large No. 6 or No. 8 Spin-N-Glo, might do well. The big drift bobber's whirling and dipping actions would definitely excite and attract the fish. The only drawback is getting a proper drift on the large boulder bottom. This method is my second choice.

A fisherman armed with a 2/5, 3/4 or 1 ounce oval, classic or elongated style spoon is well equipped to go after trophy steelhead in this type water. The spoon's concentrated weight and style allows it to sink quickly and flutter while being slowly worked over the top of the tackle eating boulders. Remember also that a spoon, to a degree, resembles a small fish. Giant steelhead are at the top of the river's pecking order. By being the largest fish, they are extremely territorial and will remove any intruders to their holding spot, smaller fish and spoons inclusive. Most importantly, and this is the main reason a 20- pound-plus trophy steelhead will strike a spoon, the spoon's large profile combined with its flash excites and/or angers a big fish, and that excitement will make him move his ponderous bulk to strike.

Besides the trophies I've been fortunate enough to tangle with, I've also been privileged to be around another dozen when hooked by others. Out of these dozen, 10 were taken on spoons, one on drift gear, and one on a diving plug. Every one of those 20-pound beasts came from the water type described earlier—all areas were seven to fifteen feet deep. If you are still looking for Number One, concentrating on areas with depth (the most important ingredient), boulder bottoms, and a choppy surface will put you in touch. Note that over the years I have spent the majority of time drift fishing—about a 75/25 split. Yet 95 percent of my trophy steelhead were taken on spoons. No coincidence—conclusive evidence.

Of course, fishing the right water with the right method means nothing if there are no big fish present. Get to know one river system intimately, and learn when the bulk of the larger steelhead arrive. Please note that trophy steelhead are usually male native fish, and 20 pound or better specimens are rare, no matter what river system you happen to fish. Use your best judgement when landing one, and remember that a phcto will preserve your trophy longer and will look better than a wall mount. Most importantly, a released giant will produce more big fish like itself.

If I have not yet convinced you of the spoon's prowess on trophy steelhead, here is one final thought to ponder. My friend, Pierce Clegg, is owner/operations manager of Norlakes Lodge on the Babine River on the Skeena system in British Columbia. The Skeena and its tributaries, most notably the Bulkley, Babine, Kispiox and Sustut, are home to the largest steelhead in the world. (These rivers are currently under catch and release status.) Twenty-pound-plus steelhead, while not common anywhere, are hooked up here with greater frequency than on any other river system in the Pacific drainage. Pierce keeps close tabs on his river, and that includes which technique each of his guests use and the size of the steelhead they catch. He also compares notes with other lodge owners on the Babine and other Skeena tributaries. Year after year, one style of lure is responsible for the largest steelhead landed in each camp, on each river. That lure, ladies and gentlemen, is the spoon.

Not an uncommon sight when visiting the trophy steelhead rivers of northern British Columbia. This 24 lb. giant buck poses in the midst of a late October snowstorm.

Chapter 3
Techniques For Fishing The Spoon

As with any style of steelhead fishing, spoon fishing requires the use of different techniques for varying situations and river conditions. Just as a fly fisherman would not use the same lines, casts or flies, or a drift fisherman the same amount of lead or size/color of drift bobber, the spoon fisherman must adjust his technique for present conditions.

In this chapter, we will discuss the importance of correct spoon technique – not just proper spoon choice and presentation to steelhead under specific river conditions, but techniques to insure that your spoon is always working properly at the right depth, speed, and angle.

Remember, knowledge of proper spoon technique is your gateway to success when spoon fishing for steelhead. Before spoon color, weight or style is even a factor, you must be able to apply the correct technique to existing conditions.

Drift Naturally And Avoid "The Push"

Beginning and veteran steelheaders often share a common misconception about spoons. They believe the new spoon they just recently took out of its bubble packaging and cast into the river will sink, and sink quickly, because it is made of metal. The result is the spoon is fished improperly, the angler overlooking the overwhelming laws of physics.

A spoon simply cast out and reeled in will be lifted to the surface by water force, not unlike a water skier being pulled upwards on takeoff. This incorrect assumption of the spoon's weight automatically keeping it near or on the bottom means the steelheader will be basically fishing just under the surface, resulting in the spoon being out of the fish's vision window. After fishing just below the surface film unsuccessfully with spoons, frustration usually sets in and the fisherman inevitable reverts back to bait and drift gear. Another lure convert lost to "the push." Avoiding "the push" is one of the keys to successful spoon fishing in rivers for steelhead.

The first step to keep your spoon from "pushing" up to the surface is to drift naturally with the existing river currents. Most steelhead spoons are designed to perform at optimum action in light or zero current. That means, because of designs, when greater than normal force is run against the spoon, the spoon will plane, or "push" toward the surface. In other words, if you just cast the spoon out on a tight line and allow the current to take over, it will spin past its speed threshold and spin to the surface. Since most spoons, believe it or not, are not

Winter steelheading is not always a ritual performed in wool and raingear. Although the mornings can be frosty, an afternoon on a West Coast river on a sunny winter day can be quite pleasant.

designed to perform at their best in swift flowing water, you the steelheader must adjust the speed of the presentation to allow it to work naturally.

Never add lead above the spoon to negate the push. It destroys the feel of the spoon's action to the rod tip, and makes for an unnatural presentation. Repeat, never add lead!

The idea is to keep enough tension on the line to allow the spoon to work properly with existing currents, yet not so much that it causes the spoon to rise. This is done by adjustments in rod angle. Positioning of your rod is what dictates the speed and depth of your spoon through a drift.

After your cast enters the water, allow the spoon to sink, while keeping absolute minimum tension on the line. A perfect compromise is line tight enough to almost pull the spoon out of position, yet enough line belly so that each "thump" of the working spoon can be seen in the movement of the line. By keeping the line tight, no excess line is caught in the current to unnecessarily speed up the drift.

Follow the working spoon downriver with the rod tip, at or slightly slower than present current speed. How high or low to position the rod will depend on the depth of the holding water. The deeper the run, the lower to the water the rod tip should be held to allow the spoon to work at maximum depth. The shallower the run, the higher the rod tip, to allow for more "push" on the spoon and greater pressure on the line to keep the spoon from sinking.

When the spoon has hit river bottom, or has reached required depth, hold the rod tip stationary or raise it slightly to again allow the spoon to rise and continue working and travelling downstream with the current. Soon after the spoon rises and begins to work, there will be a point where you must again follow it downstream with the rod tip to allow it to sink into the steelhead's range of vision. You may also want to feed line in quick, short lengths to keep the spoon near the bottom.

After gaining experience, you will begin to develop a "sixth sense" of knowing exactly what your spoon is doing and where it is in the drift. You will be able to keep it near the bottom, yet moving along slightly above it. It is the ability to make the spoon rise and drop during a drift that will set you apart from other steelheaders.

How many times this is done in a single drift depends on the size of the piece of holding water you are fishing. It doesn't matter if you have repeated this once or a dozen or more times while covering the water, there will be a point at the end of the drift where the current is no longer strong enough to suspend the spoon. This usually happens when the spoon has completed its swing and is beneath you. Since the spoon is normally now at the shallowest part of the drift, hold the rod tip high and pointing slightly upstream from where you stand to allow for maximum "push" against the lure and line. At the same time reel in line and work the spoon as slow as possible back toward you. Many steelhead will follow

The four major commercial and practical designs. (left to right) The fat/teardrop, the oval, the classic, and the elongated.

the spoon and hit it when it is slowly worked back upstream like this, especially in wintertime (36-46 degree) water conditions.

While each bit of holding water is different in depth, current speed, width, and length, a general rule of thumb can be practiced. As stated earlier, to make the spoon run deeper, lower the rod tip and follow the spoon downriver at current speed. To make it run shallower, hold the rod tip higher and swing your rod tip against the current upriver. How much rod angle is dependant on the present river situation, and this can only be judged by on the river experience. The guidelines to work with I can supply here, but as it's been said, practice makes perfect.

Drifting naturally by using correct rod angle to avoid "the push" is not the only reason to do so. Not allowing the spoon to rise prevents it from spinning. Spoons are designed to wobble, not spin. When steelheading, it is paramount that the spoon, regardless of design, wobbles and spin is kept to a minimum. That is one of the most important rules of spoon fishing. There are two excellent reasons for doing this.

When the spoon starts to spin, usually due to pulling the spoon against the current when it is not necessary, its capacity for buoyancy increases with each revolution. This causes planing upward, or "the push." While maintaining wobble to decrease push is necessary, it is not the only reason. When a spoon wobbles, it gives off a higher percentage of flash than when it spins. The more flash, the wider of an area a steelhead can see the lure. In wintertime, when steelhead are typically lethargic due to cold water, maximum flash is needed to excite them into striking. More attraction, more steelhead. Simple.

Since about 95 percent of the time your spoon is not visible (by you) while it is working underwater, how do you know if it is working properly? The key is your rod tip. Some anglers pay little or no attention to the action of their rod tip, they figure as long as it is "wiggling," the spoon is doing something to attract fish. These are probably the same fishermen that assume the spoon will automatically sink. It is a steady, "thump-thump-thump" that is desired to make sure the spoon is working properly. By slow I mean your rod tip should pulse or dip three to six times per second on the average. This "thump" telegraphs to you what the spoon is doing when travelling underwater. The slow "thump" tells you the spoon is wobbling as desired. A rapid vibration and deep flexing of the rod tip means the spoon is spinning, adding to the push and lessening its attraction capabilities.

Don't be discouraged if your spoon is spinning. In some situations it is unavoidable because of positioning. Better to fish a spinning spoon than not fish the area at all. A spinning spoon will still attract steelhead, that is a fact, but in the majority of situations it reduces the spoon's effectiveness. Later on in this chapter, you will see where spoon spin is desirable in certain situations. But, in order to avoid "the push," spoon spin must be kept to a minimum. By drifting naturally, using correct rod angle, and making the spoon wobble and not spin, you can keep "the push" out of your streamside vocabulary.

Position Yourself Properly

The importance of proper positioning on the river is directly related to how much success you will have when spoon fishing for steelhead. It is positioning that sets average steelheaders apart from excellent ones. And because you are spoon fishing, you will be looking at holding water much differently than a bait, fly, spinner or plug fisherman. As you will read, positioning not only is important in presenting the spoon, but also determines what side of the river to fish, and what section to be on.

The first rule of proper positioning on the river is putting yourself on a spot at the uppermost section of the holding water you are fishing. This means you will always be working downstream. It doesn't matter if the stretch of water is one or one hundred feet long, make

This twenty-two pound Skeena system buck was taken in holding water that had all the important ingredients for trophy-sized steelhead: deep water, boulder bottom, and choppy surface. A one ounce, fast sinking elongated style was irresistible.

your first cast just above the area where you would expect the first steelhead to be holding under the current conditions, and let the spoon swing downstream to that area. Remember, spoons are at their peak effectiveness when cast straight out or slightly downstream and allowed to swing toward the side of the river you are on. This is how you should begin every cast.

There are three very important reasons for starting at the top of the drift and working down. First, and this is one of the most critical keys to spoon success, it allows the spoon to be worked in front of the steelhead. By letting the spoon swing in front of the fish, it can see the spoon easier, because the steelhead's greatest range of vision is directly in front of it. Two, steelhead are territorial creatures. The spoon wobbling downstream into its "space" will be treated like any smaller fish in the river's pecking order, attacked and subsequently removed. Three, there is no chance your line or spoon will be dragged across the body of the steelhead from its blind side. This would obviously spook the hell out of the fish. This is what commonly happens when casting is begun in a random part of the holding water, or a fisherman casts the spoon at an upstream angle. You must start at the very top (upstream) portion of the drift and work down. That way every fish (or the only fish) in that section will have the spoon presented in front of them every time. And yes, it is a lot of work, but it is the only way to do it, believe me. Random casting leaves too much to chance, and you will only catch the random fish.

Before you make that first cast, you must determine how far above the top part of the holding water to stand, or anchor your boat. This is where you have to make a mental gauge of a "workable casting distance." First, keep in mind that you want to fish the shortest possible amount of line and still be able to cover the water. If the area you intend to fish is on the other side of the river, too far to cast and control line comfortably, if possible go to the other side. By fishing comfortably I mean having no more line out than you can control immediately. Second, the less line that is out, the less that is in the water, and that is less line drag to unnecessarily speed up your drift. It is also easier to tell what the spoon is doing—feel is not lost due to line stretch.

Always get as close as conditions allow to your target water. Position your drift boat or yourself close to the water you will be working (within the boundaries of safe wading) but far enough away as not to spook steelhead. Since there are no two drifts on any river that are exactly alike, only you can judge your starting point at the top of the drift and how close to get to your target by experience. That sounds like a cop-out, but because of different personalities of each bit of holding water, there is no way to describe "how to" precisely. The best rule of thumb is to always start at the top part of the holding water. Always.

Positioning yourself properly also has a lot to do with where and how you will be fishing on the river that particular day. Don't just jump in the truck and drive to the river to fish random areas. Before you leave, draw up a mental plan of the area you intend to fish and what spoon technique will work best for the conditions that day. Planning ahead will take away most of the guesswork, and let you concentrate totally on techniques you planned to use. Professional athletes, most notably football players, would never go into competition without a solid game plan. Failure to do so would be a losing proposition. The same can be said for a steelheader that fishes randomly. You will be shut out many more times than you score.

Remember, proper positioning is knowing where to stand or anchor at the uppermost section of the fishable water to begin a presentation, how far away to gauge a workable casting distance, keeping as much line out of the water as is comfortably possible, and drawing up a plan of where and what technique to use that day on the river. Combine these with persistence, an open mind, and on the river experience and you will be one step closer to becoming a successful spoon fisherman.

PRESENTING THE SPOON

Fisherman "A" is positioned properly at the uppermost section of holding water to start the presentation and begin working the drift. The initial cast should always be straight across from the angler or slightly downstream, to start the spoon working immediately at optimum action and to keep the presentation slow. How much angle across or down to begin the cast depends on current speed and depth. The more depth and speed, the straighter across the cast should be to allow the spoon to sink into the steelhead's range of vision. The slower or shallower the drift, the more downstream angle needed. At this great angle "the push" is increased and prevents the spoon from sinking too quickly.

The number 1 through 6 suggest how many casts it could take to thoroughly work a section of holding water. The number of casts in one position will vary on each river and drift. This number will depend on river size, width of holding water, and degree of visibility. For example, two feet of visibility, two feet between casts, five feet of visibility, five feet between casts, etc.

The imaginary line between A[1] and "B" is where the initial cast to begin a drift should land. Point "B" is also where the spoon should first come in contact with or be near the bottom. "B" is also the point where the spoon will be in the steelhead's vision window, where the drift first starts to slow, and the spoon will be working at optimum action and presentation speed.

When all holding water has been worked properly for the conditions in one position, step downriver to a new position and begin casting again. How far downstream to step depends again on degree of visibility—two feet of visibility, step two feet downstream, five feet of visibility, step five feet down, etc. Be sure to overlap casting area (position C) so no fish will be spooked by walking down or positioning the boat too far between the end of the previous position's drift to the start of the new one. This way, no fish is missed. Repeat casting and move down until all holding water is worked.

24

"Driftmending" The Spoon

I once wrote an article for *Salmon Trout Steelheader* magazine about a technique called "driftmending." It is a combination of fly fishing and drift gear fishing used to present a bait/bobber at a much slower speed than a normal drift. After using this technique for a few years, I found it to be just as deadly when incorporated with spoon fishing.

This idea was spawned, so to speak, on Washington's Skykomish River during the catch and release season. I was fortunate enough to watch two very talented fly guys work a riffle. What struck me was the amount of time it took for them to complete each drift. Considering the speed of the water they were fishing, it was much longer than I thought was possible with fly gear. (I was not a fly fisherman at that time.) It was the technique they were using that lit the bulb over my head.

They would repeatedly cast slightly downstream from their position, immediately making as many line mends as necessary to keep the line taught and straight downriver from rod tip to fly. The rods were held at full arm extension, away from the body. Before the fly would start to rise out of the steelhead's window of vision, they would turn slowly downriver, following the drift, keeping the same tension on the line for the entire presentation until they stripped in and re-cast. By doing this the riffle was fished at the same speed, slightly slower than the holding water current, start to finish. The reason they could present the fly slowly through the entire drift was the immediate mending of the line to alleviate drag that speeds up the drift.

As I watched them cast, I wondered if anyone had applied this technique to drift fishing. The premise was

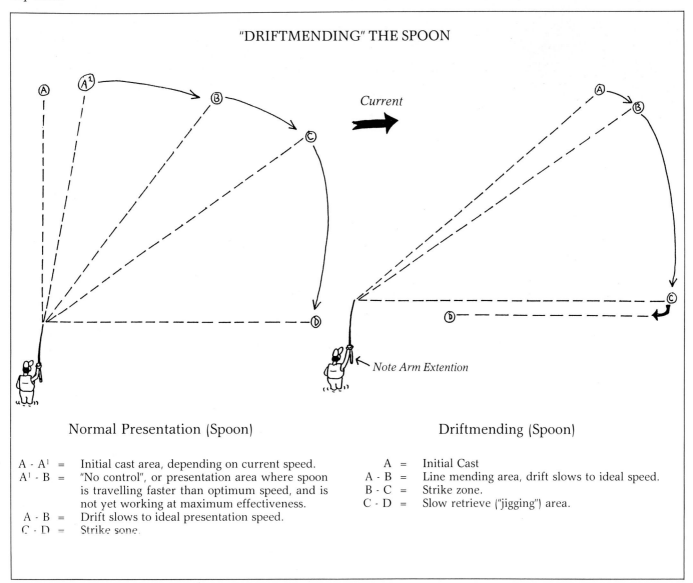

"DRIFTMENDING" THE SPOON

Current

Note Arm Extention

Normal Presentation (Spoon)

A - A¹	=	Initial cast area, depending on current speed.
A¹ - B	=	"No control", or presentation area where spoon is travelling faster than optimum speed, and is not yet working at maximum effectiveness.
A - B	=	Drift slows to ideal presentation speed.
C - D	=	Strike sone.

Driftmending (Spoon)

A	=	Initial Cast
A - B	=	Line mending area, drift slows to ideal speed.
B - C	=	Strike zone.
C - D	=	Slow retrieve ("jigging") area.

Trophy steelhead prefer a slow, deep, animated lure. With driftmending it is much easier to keep the spoon working in front of the fish longer, therefore giving large, scrutinous, or lethargic steelhead an "extra look."

so basic, to mend monofilament line, keeping the drift slow and in complete control throughout the holding water, not just at the end when it finally slows in the current break. I naturally wanted to find out if this idea was even practical. When incorporated with spoons I found this technique to be best during typical winter or early summer snowmelt conditions, where higher, cloudy, or colder water dictates a slower presentation of the spoon to increase effectiveness.

To "driftmend," I would suggest using a level-wind reel for maximum effectiveness and flexibility. This doesn't mean you cannot use a spinning reel. It is necessary when driftmending to be able to give line in quick, short lengths to stay near the bottom. It is just easier to give line with a level-wind than a spinning reel.

When "driftmending," your casts will always be downstream from where you stand or anchor; how much of an angle depends on current speed. The slower the current, the greater the angle downstream you must cast. After your spoon enters the water, stay on the reel at the beginning of the drift, giving out line in quick, short lengths to keep in contact with the bottom or at desired depth, at the same time staying on the fine line of keeping all slack out the mono to allow the spoon to flutter on the fall.

Hold the rod straight out, away from your body with a full arm extension. The rod should be almost horizontal with the tip pointing to 10 o'clock. From this position,

when the spoon starts to work downstream you can easily "mend" or "flip" the monofilament like a fly fisherman mends his fly line, keeping a straight line from rod tip to spoon. Be sure to reel up any slack between mends. By doing this you are not allowing any slack line to drag in the current and speed up the drift. After you have made the desired number of mends to slow your drift, stay in the same position and turn your upper body slowly downriver, following the spoon, always keeping the line straight between rod tip and lure.

When your drift is at its end and your line is below you, your spoon will want to sink to the bottom in the slower water. When this happens, raise the rod tip to 12 o'clock to make the spoon rise. Reel in slowly, at the same time raising and lowering the rod slightly to literally "jig" the spoon back to your position. Many steelhead in higher water will follow your jigged spoon and take a few feet off the rod tip. By making the same distance cast and moving down through the holding water in two to three foot sections, every bit of the drift will thoroughly covered with the spoon.

What "driftmending" does is keep the spoon working (slower than the current, about 1/2 to 3/4 speed) at the same speed from first contact with the bottom after the cast to the tail end of the drift. To do it correctly, I've found that a heavier than normal spoon for the conditions is sometimes a necessity, and I'll explain why. The heavier spoon makes holding the bottom easier; the increased weight neutralizes "the push" and allows for a slower drift. For example, if you were using a 1/2-ounce spoon for the conditions, jump up to a 3/4 ounce. Sometimes it will take twice as long to cover the water. In high, colored, or cold water it effectively doubles the chance for a hookup, giving lethargic and scrutinous steelhead extra time to find and strike the spoon. When fishing low, clear flows, in most situation a normal weighted spoon will hold bottom just fine – the need to jump to a heavier one is not necessary. The key is, when fishing slower, the longer a lure is in front of a steelhead, the more likely it is to strike.

For "driftmending," my first choice is an elongated style spoon and a classic or oval style my second. The elongated has the least surface to weight ratio, which means it works deep easier, with a lot of action when worked slowly. The classic style should be driftmended in shallower or slower water than the elongated. The classic is the best style to driftmend in fast riffles for summer steelhead. Your spoon choice will be made on the river.

By fishing slower with this technique, you will invariably hook fish that others using more swiftly presented techniques did not get a shot at. You will lose fewer spoons on a tight, downstream line, it does not get a chance to settle in the rocks, unless you want it to. (See Ringing The Dinner Bell in this chapter.) The bottom line here is increased hookups. Instead of effectively covering only about 40 percent of the drift at the optimum desired speed (where your spoon slows naturally in the slower current break), you will be fishing at 80 percent of optimum desired spoon speed.

Note that large, trophy steelhead prefer a slow, deliberate presentation, so driftmending is definitely the best way to pursue the giant rainbow. My largest fish, a 27-pound buck, was driftmended with a spoon.

"Driftmending" with spoons is a bit more difficult than doing it with drift gear. But if it sounds like a tough technique to master, it really isn't, and with some practice anyone can do it. If you give driftmending a good long test, especially in high, cloudy, fast, or cold water, you will have a helpful edge when spoon fishing.

Back-Trolling The Spoon

The word "back-trolling" immediately conjures up visions of diving plugs being skillfully worked by the oarsman, easing his drift boat down a deep, classic slot of holding water. Back-trolling is not exclusive to drift boaters pulling plugs. Before the turn of the 20th century, Great Britain and East coast Atlantic salmon fishermen employed a technique called "harling," which in essence was back-trolling on rivers with weighted salmon flies positioned downstream, below the boat. Today bait fishermen use diving planers and assorted diving plugs to back-troll a spinning drift bobber/bait combination downstream into steelhead holding water. Spoon fishermen on today's rivers can also use the back-trolling technique.

Fat/teardrop style spoons are often ideal for backtrolling because their wide profile makes them the most buoyant style spoon. This 18 lb. March native buck took a backtrolled teardrop. Brad Bailey photo.

There are some major restrictions when attempting to back-troll spoons. Because a spoon is not buoyant like a diving plug, the angler must constantly adjust line tension when easing it downstream, using "the push" to its fullest to keep the spoon suspended and working off the bottom. This is difficult to do. It requires practice to get the "feel" of walking a spoon back down the current. You must be able to give line in short amounts to allow the spoon to inch downstream. This means when fishing out of a drift boat, you must hang onto the rod and work the spoon instead of letting the river do it, like a plug. And, because it takes a lot of "push" to keep the spoon buoyant and able to be backed straight downstream, your spoon will be spinning like crazy. As discussed earlier, a wobbling spoon is preferred over a spinning spoon, but steelhead will still strike a stationary, spinning spoon.

You are probably asking, why back-troll the spoon? When spoon fishing, especially from the bank, there are three situations when back-trolling will be your choice of spoon technique.

The first situation is encountered on small to medium sized streams where the river makes a split around an island. Here the water comes back together and slams against itself, creating a seam at the point the two waters meet. Steelhead will sit from the tip of the island at the top of the seam, along the entire seam's length until it shallows up or disappears. Because the water is flowing fast on both sides, this type of spot is almost impossible to fish with a spoon using regular techniques. You need to stand on the point of the island (by safely wading to it or beaching your drift boat and walking to it) directly above the seam and back-troll the spoon right down the middle of its entire length. When back-trolling the seams, use a classic style spoon. The classic style's near perfect balance of surface area to weight makes it the easiest to use in this situation. It creates a happy medium between "the push" and sinking too quickly.

The second situation is encountered on small streams. By my definition "small" streams are from 10 to 20 feet across. When bank fishing small water you frequently find yourself on the wrong side of the river to make a proper presentation. This means the deepest, fastest flow is on your side. On small streams, this fast, deep water only reaches out from a few to six feet. A spoon cast out over into the slower water would only have a few feet to work before the line catches in the swift water in front of you, sweeping the spoon swiftly downriver and to the surface. This gives the steelhead no chance to get to it. Since most steelhead rods are between 8 and 9 feet long, reaching out to a back-trolling position in small streams is relatively simple.

Position yourself properly at the top of the holding water, with your rod in front of you over the water in the 10 o'clock position. Back-troll the spoon down the current edge, where the fast water starts to slow. Steelhead will hold in that 12 inch strip of current break, in the transition line. Because the water in the current edge in small streams is slow and relatively shallow, a fat teardrop style spoon works best. With this style "the push" is at its maximum, which will make keeping the spoon suspended while backing it downstream easier. You don't have to pass these areas up on small streams just because you are on the "wrong side."

The third situation is when you encounter an area where you spot a steelhead practically rubbing his nose against an underwater obstruction. The fish will not be able to see a bait or lure zipping by, because it has its face buried on the rock, tree, etc. The only way to pluck out these nose-buried fish is to back-troll a lure directly alongside the obstruction, as close to the fish's head as possible.

Current will usually be moving at a good clip near the obstruction. This means with the stiffer current "the push" will be at its maximum. Use an elongated or oval spoon for increased depth in this situation. Position yourself directly above the obstruction, either by safely wading or anchoring. Because of the decreased area of vision around the steelhead, you will literally be holding the spoon alongside the fish's head, stationary in the current. In order to keep the spoon down, in many cases you may have to shove the rod tip down into the water a foot or so. The steelhead (hopefully) will peel away from the spot and strike the spoon when it can see it. This technique will pay off for the hard work because no one else (except plug fishermen) will have a shot as these fish but you.

You may be thinking, why can't I just use a diving plug in the last two river situations instead of a spoon? You can, and they definitely work better than spoons in those situations. What if you have no plugs with you? If you are carrying some spoons, you don't have to pass up the water. And remember, with spoon fishing or any other steelheading technique, if you are ever going to be an expert, you must learn to fish with your method in all possible situations. Only when you have exhausted all your options of technique should you switch to a different, more effective one. Never lose sight of the fact that there is always one method that will outfish another in a given condition. Back-trolling is just an important part of the full circle of spoon fishing for steelhead.

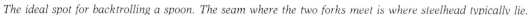

The ideal spot for backtrolling a spoon. The seam where the two forks meet is where steelhead typically lie.

Ringing The Dinner Bell

This section and the one following (Jigging the Unfishable Water) should have been included in Chapter 2, "Why Spoons Over Other Methods?", because here we will be discussing an advantage that only spoons can give you. It is, however, more of a technique; that's why it's in this chapter. As the title suggests, this technique uses the spoon to send an audio signal to the steelhead.

Late summer/early fall low-water summer steelhead, like this one being released by Mike Cronen, often go into non-biting doldrums. Adding sound to sight will often trigger a strike from these "buried" fish.

Sound travels well underwater. It can be an added attractor to any lure. Consider the effectiveness of the Hot Shot style plug with the built-in rattle. It's a fact, sound, or more specifically the right sound, attracts steelhead. You can make the spoon literally "ring" by making it bounce repeatedly off the rocks during the drift.

To do this, you have to allow the spoon to hit bottom with a little more frequency than normal. During a normal drift the spoon will make bottom contact several times. Each time the spoon hits a rock it "dings." So, instead of hitting bottom, say, three times per drift, let it make contact six to seven times.

The plus side to this technique is when fishing in winter or early spring snowmelt conditions, when the water is in the high 30's to low 40 degree range. The sound from the spoon combined with the flash can "wake up" lethargic steelhead. This also works on occasion in very low water, late summer conditions when steelhead have been holding in a spot for an extended period. The noise from the dinging spoon will sometimes cause these stale fish to hit.

The minus side is that by letting the spoon come in contact with the bottom two to three times the norm in a drift, snags and lost lures will increase, and hook(s) will dull faster. However, by always keeping tension on the line and reacting quickly to each "ding," snags and lost lures will be kept to a minimum, and some filing to re-sharpen your hook is all the extra work that's needed.

If your spoon does hang up on a rock, don't just pull on the snag until the line snaps. There is a way to get 75 percent of rock snags back. Since a hook point cannot penetrate rock, the only thing holding your spoon to the rock is tight line. First feed five or six feet of line out to create a line belly below the snagged spoon. Then a swift striking motion with your rod will cause a downstream pull on the line belly, pulling the spoon in the opposite direction away from the snag.

I would suggest only using this technique when you know or suspect steelhead are present and have refused every other spoon technique, otherwise it could get expensive. But when steelhead go into doldrums, adding sound to sight might just be the ticket.

Jigging The "Unfishable" Water

This next technique is admittedly one you will rarely use, but will produce steelhead in areas that the majority of fishermen deem unfishable. Your river(s) may or may not contain stretches of water similar to the ones described here. Should you ever encounter a situation like this, you will have an effective spoon technique to use.

Unusually deep holes, common in canyon stretches where there is no conventional holding water for steelhead to rest, present a real challenge. This water usually has steep, high rock walls surrounding it, can be 20 or more feet deep and characteristically has slicks,

up-boils and varying currents. Because of haphazard currents and unusual depth, this type of water can only be fished at low flow. In this water, a steelheader has two options when choosing a technique.

One, he can choose drift gear. By adding enough lead, bottom can be reached and bait can be presented to these deep-water fish. However, the amount of line out combined with swirling, ever changing currents makes detecting a subtle pickup difficult—not impossible, but difficult. The exaggerated amount of weight needed to get down to the fish would normally frighten them in the clear water. This setup does take steelhead in these conditions (I know, I used it for years), but it is not the only option, or the most effective.

The second option is to "jig" them out with a spoon. In order to jig a spoon you need to be directly above the water you intend to work. In canyon holes, normally the only casting position is directly above the holding water. Ideally, you want to position yourself on a high point or ledge over the hole, on top of some large streamside boulders, or anywhere that fits these descriptions. You want to keep as close to a 90 degree angle from rod tip to spoon as possible.

Washington's Olympic Peninsula has many rivers that flow through canyon stretches like this one. Breathtaking in their beauty, but difficulty in access and fishability make them lonely places.

The author stings a late summer steelhead. This fish was jigged out of a fifteen foot deep hole with a one half ounce elongated spoon.

To "jig," you need a spoon style that flutters exceptionally well when worked vertically. An elongated style spoon is the choice here – the Krocodile by Luhr Jensen or the Mepps' Syclops work best. Remember, surface area is minimal, so this style spoon sinks the fastest and its design is for maximum action vertically, perfect for jigging. Steelhead in these deep holes are often suspended and not sitting on the bottom, so be sure to work the hole from surface to bottom.

To "jig," work the elongated spoon in the same way you would jig for salmon out on the saltchuck. This is the one time you will want to cast slightly upstream to begin the presentation. To get the spoon positioned directly below, you have to cast upstream. After the cast, hold the rod in the 12 o'clock position, from there you can drop the tip sharply approximately a foot to start the spoon fluttering on a free-fall. Then from 9 o'clock to almost straight down follow the spoon's descent with the rod tip. Let out a few feet of line, raise the rod tip back to 12 o'clock, and repeat until you reach bottom and/or worked the entire hole.

What type of finish to use depends on what time of year you are fishing. In the winter, use a nickel or silver plate. In summer, go with a brass finish. (See Chapters 4 and 5 for explanations of seasonal spoon color choice.) And, because the water is very deep and has changing currents, a heavy spoon will be necessary. Your on the river judgement will tell you what weight jig to use – 3/4 to one ounce should be plenty. Be ready for a strike at any position of the presentation, a steelhead will take on the down-flutter as well as when the spoon is worked back toward the surface.

As stated earlier, you may use this technique only on the rare occasion, but it makes the "unfishable" (and ignored by other steelheaders) deep-water holes a target area for jigging spoons.

Types Of Strikes And Setting The Hook

It is inevitable — once you get comfortable with your newfound techniques, and stay persistent, steelhead strikes will soon follow. You must be familiarized with the different types of steelhead strikes, and how to react to each one. That first contact with a steelhead is truly the most exciting part of steelheading. With spoons, you will typically experience three kinds of strikes, and each one requires a different angler reaction.

The first and most common strike is what I call the "slam dunk." These are extremely exciting, arm-wrenching, rod-flattening yanks that no fisherman would have a problem detecting. This strike is the one most commonly associated with spoon fishing, but I estimate it only occurs 50 percent of the time. Steelhead that take a spoon this hard have already driven most of the hook point into their mouths, but not the barb, especially if the point finds a bony plate. When fish strike hard it is easy to forget to set the hook. A firm, upward lift of the rod immediately after the strike (before the steelhead goes ape and shakes the hook out) will insure a solid hook-set.

If the cast is like pulling the pin on the grenade, then the strike is the explosion. This winter run tailwalks in an unsuccessful attempt at throwing the hook.

The second type of strike is the "stop." There is nothing too exciting about this take. The spoon will simply halt its drift, not unlike it does when it hangs up on a rock or branch. Ultra-skilled steelheaders can detect the ever so slight movement that telegraphs "fish" and not "snag" to the rod tip. Most fishermen do not possess that sixth sense, and even the seasoned vets cannot tell a strike from a snag in most cases when the spoon "stops." The old steelheading adage rings loudly here, "jerk or be one." When in doubt, set the hook! Many times it will be a rock, but occasionally the "rock" will respond with heavy head shakes.

When a steelhead "stops" the spoon, it either has the body of the spoon or just the point of the hook in its mouth. On this type of strike, immediately after the stop, set the hook as hard as your setup allows. Again, don't give the steelhead a chance to realize it has something foreign in its mouth and reject it. You need to "rip lip," "adjust his dental work," and "cross his eyes"!

The third type of strike is the most infrequent and unusual. It is one of those "what the heck happened there" occurrences you may be familiar with. This kind of take happens when your spoon is at the end of its swing in a drift or is directly below you, hanging straight down in the current. Your rod tip will suddenly go "light." The line goes instantly limp as if the line was swiftly cut. What has happened is a steelhead has taken the spoon and quickly swam upstream toward your position. About half of these fish are lost because of the instant slack line created. I realize this is easier said than done, but when the rod tip goes "light" like this, get on the reel immediately and take up the slack line as rapidly as possible. When the line finally tightens (if the fish is still there), hit him as hard as your gear will allow. It too will only have the point of the hook penetrating its mouth, so a hard hook set is necessary.

All this talk of properly detecting strikes and hook-setting isn't worth the life of a sea lion if you don't use a razor sharp hook. No hook, and I repeat, no hook, regardless of manufacturer's claims, is sharp enough out of its packaging for immediate use. Claims of laser this, razor that, and needle-sharp blah-blah are nothing more than great marketing catch phrases. They all need to be sharpened. A diamond sharpener or hook file is as important as any other piece of gear you carry on the river, if not the most important. Check that hook(s) every other cast to insure it stays super-sharp. A rock can dull a hook point easily without you even realizing it.

Absolute sharpness is critical in hooking steelhead that "stop" the spoon or take it "light." It is the ultra-sharp point that sticks in the steelhead's mouth that allows you the split second of grace before you can set the hook. A sticky-sharp hook also makes for easier penetration into a steelhead's hard, bony mouth. Hooks that aren't sharpened and kept sharp equal lost fish.

Plunking The Thin-Bladed Spoon

In Chapter 4 (winter steelhead) the "Green Means Go" section states that spoons are not effective in restricted visibility conditions (less than two feet.) True, any less visibility and a steelhead cannot find or follow a moving lure. What if there was a way to fish the spoon effectively in a stationary position? Sounds like plunking, doesn't it? Right. Plunking the spoon can be an effective, yet admittedly boring, technique to use in water conditions slightly too high for conventional spoon techniques.

During wintertime conditions, when rivers are starting to drop after being high, brown and roily, there will be a period when the river will have one to two feet of visibility. This condition is a tease; there is enough visibility to fish, but not enough to drift spoons. This is also the time, when water begins to change from brown to green, that steelhead start to move upstream. Plunking time. To "plunk" the spoon requires a special setup with a very different style spoon in a specific type of water.

First, to understand why the plunking rig is effective, a look at the style of target water is in order. In any stretch of holding water, there will be what is called a current break, or a "transition line." This line is a thin strip of water that separates fast flowing water from slow moving slack water. This line is normally only a few feet wide. When entering rivers, anadromous fish (steelhead, salmon, trout) follow the contour of the river banks upstream along the transition lines. During this brown/green high water period, steelhead will be moving (providing the river is above 40 degrees) upstream at a quickened pace. When fish are on the move, any regular steelheading technique is an iffy proposition, the chances of an advancing steelhead locating your travelling offering in the limited visibility are remote at best. Your best bet is to place your lure in the transition line and allow the fish to swim right into it.

Plunking the transition line requires a very different breed of spoon, the thin-blade trolling style. Thin bladed spoons work best for plunking because their ultra-thin

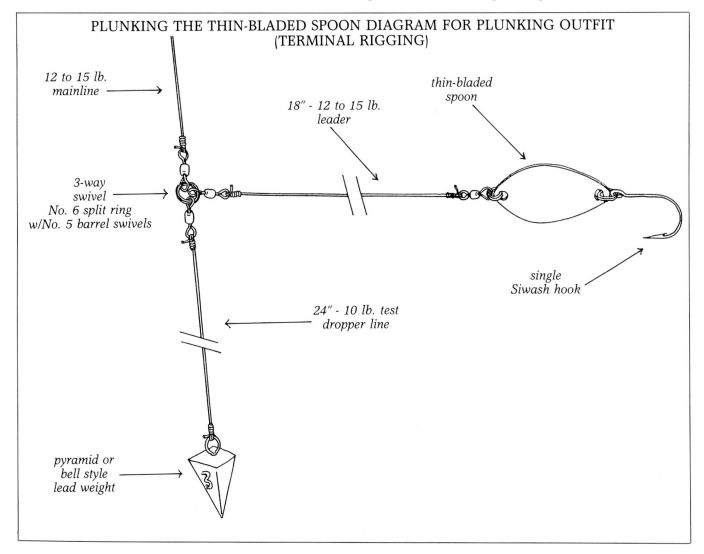

PLUNKING THE THIN-BLADED SPOON DIAGRAM FOR PLUNKING OUTFIT
(TERMINAL RIGGING)

12 to 15 lb. mainline

thin-bladed spoon

18" - 12 to 15 lb. leader

3-way swivel
No. 6 split ring w/No. 5 barrel swivels

single Siwash hook

24" - 10 lb. test dropper line

pyramid or bell style lead weight

profile causes almost neutral buoyancy when held stationary in the current. They weigh practically nothing (1/8 ounce), and their thin bodies are ten times less resistant to water, characteristics that make them work at an accelerated action, much faster than regular casting style spoons. Their quick, fluttering, darting actions make them deadly plunking lures.

Because visibility is only one to two feet, a thin-blade spoon with a bright, highly visible finish is an obvious choice. Spoons with a glow in the dark paint on the convex side work best with matte silver plate or matte silver/chartreuse head running a close second. Color pattern is not important, it is the bright colors and finishes that attract steelhead in these low-visibility conditions.

An angler jigging a deep, boiling canyon hole for summer runs. Positioning above the target water like this is necessary to properly work the spoon.

Now that water type and spoon style/color have been established, you must use a rig that presents the lure properly to the steelhead. Start with a homemade three-way swivel. Don't use those cheap brass "T" shaped ones—they bend easily and break under pressure. Get a No. 6 split ring and three No. 5 crane barrel-type swivels and put them together. This makes a flexible, ultra-strong three-way swivel with zero weak points. Unlike the affixed commercial three-way "T" swivels, these allow total freedom of movement and a direct pull from hooked fish to the mainline.

From one of the swivels on the three way tie 18 inches of 15-pound-test leader to your flutter spoon. On the next swivel tie 24 inches of 10-pound-test dropper line to a bell-style lead sinker. Two to six ounces will suffice, depending on current strength. Tie the mainline (15 to 20 pound test) to the last remaining swivel on the three-way and you are ready to plunk.

Wintertime plunking is best in the lower sections of rivers because you will always be targeting fresh, moving steelhead. Once a "plunkable" spot has been found in the transition line, from the bank or your boat carefully place the setup in the water so the mainline, leader and dropper do not become tangled. Then slowly lower the setup down the parting line until bottom is reached. Ideal plunking depth is water from four to ten feet deep. When the sinker touches bottom, lift the rod tip and walk the setup downstream until the line is at approximately a 60 degree angle. Place the rod in a rod holder or plunking stick and tighten up the line until the sinker is just about to be lifted off the bottom. This creates a straight, tight line from sinker to rod tip. Your thin-blade spoon will be working properly when it transmits a rapid "thump-thump-thump" to the rod tip.

A diamond-shaped thin blade spoon works best for plunking. Their wide shape creates more "push" and helps support the spoon in the current. Thin-blade spoons in elongated shapes have less water resistance due to their narrower bodies, and tend to fall towards the bottom in lighter currents. The best thin-blade spoons for plunking are the No. 1 and No. 2, 1/8th and 3/16th ounce Shoffs' F.S.T., trolling style. These spoons are designed for maximum action at low trolling speeds, making them ideal for plunking. All other thin-blade trolling spoons are designed to work at high trolling speeds, making them impractical for plunking. The No. 1 and 2/0 single Siwash hooks the lures come with are perfect; they are light and do not interfere with the action or buoyancy of the spoon.

You don't have to restrict spoon plunking activities to only when rivers are too high and off colored for other spoon techniques. Plunking the thin-bladed spoons works anytime winter water conditions are up and river temperature is above 40 degrees. It is a great technique for whiling away a lazy day, and it will put you into steelhead during marginal conditions.

Chapter 4

Winter Steelhead: Silver And Cold

For the majority of the holders of steelhead permits, winter is the time to go a few rounds with the silver pugilists we all love to climb in the ring with. The sweet smell of the first high water, washing rocks clean of summer algae, combined with the snap of cold air burning the sinuses is the opiate for the steelheading masses.

I admittedly do not fish for winter steelhead as much as I used to. Every November, however, when the first snow dusts the foothills, the fever returns. In this part of the early winter, I'm inevitably drawn to the banks of the Puyallup River near my home in Tacoma, in search of hatchery steelhead. In recent years, more often than not I go home empty handed. Each time I find myself wanting to re-live the glory days of the '50s when the Puyallup was the number one steelhead producer in the state of Washington, and my late Uncle Bob was casting a spell over hundreds of them with his red/white Dardevles.

Like the Puyallup, there are many rivers in Washington that are rich in winter steelheading lore and tradition. And many of them still produce decent numbers of winter fish. I suppose it is that spirit and opportunity that drives us all to near frostbite and pneumonia in pursuit of the star of the show.

Perhaps it's the search for the cold weather icon, the 20-pound trophy. Or maybe it's the chance to view Nature's grey and leafless stark winter wardrobe. Others just want a fresh hatchery steelhead for the table. No matter what you expect from a winter fishing trip, attempting to do battle with Mr. Ironjaws is reason aplenty for being there. Fishing spoons in the winter can be a very satisfying way to experience it all.

The Cold Weather Steelhead

When to target winter steelhead depends largely on which river an angler chooses to fish. Each system is inherently different when discussing timing of fish runs. Most rivers receive the bulk of the winter run in December through February. Others get the majority of their steelhead in March, and some as late as April and May. Obviously, genetics have everything to do with which strains of fish ascend their chosen rivers during specific calendar periods. Knowing the river intimately certainly helps, and that includes which breed of steelhead you intend to pursue. I'm talking about hatchery and native steelhead.

The differences between hatchery and native winter fish are run timing, physical appearance, aggressiveness, and quality of fight. Hatchery steelhead smolts, because they are grown larger and released earlier than native smolts, mature faster and therefore return earlier than their native cousins. Late November, December and January are peak months for hatchery steelhead returns. The average size hatchery winter fish is usually six to ten pounds, or a two-salt fish, meaning two years spent at sea. Many hatcheries in Washington and other states only take the largest fish returning for broodstock; the theory behind this being larger parents,

The first snows of early winter. Mother Nature's signal that another season of cold weather steelheading is in full swing.

larger offspring. This practice has produced slightly larger hatchery steelhead on some rivers, like the Cowlitz, with a greater number of three-salt fish weighing into the teens. But still the majority of hatchery produced steelhead will be much smaller than their native brethren.

The physical appearance of a hatchery steelhead also differs from natives. The easiest way to identify a hatchery fish (winter or summer run) is by its fins. From growing up in a confined hatchery pond, fins will be bent and deformed. Dorsal and anal fins will be bent and ragged, and rays will be crooked. Tips of tails will be rounded. The Washington Department of Wildlife clips the adipose fin (the small, fleshy oval fin behind the dorsal) off when smolts are released for instant, positive identification for anglers. Other states and provinces also fin clip smolts for identification as hatchery origin.

A native winter steelhead's appearance, compared to a hatchery fish, is striking. Instead of deformed or missing fins, the native will have all fins intact and have straight, perfect rays in them. The dorsal will be tall and pointed, and so will the tips of the tail. There will be no evidence of bouncing off other fish in a confined, concrete pond.

Native steelhead make their upstream journey at different times than hatchery fish, although not quite as predictable. Natives will overlap the hatchery run in November, December and January, but these early fish are usually a few vanguards of the main run. Again, it has everything to do with each individual river system and strain of steelhead to determine peak runs of native fish. Most rivers in the Pacific drainage get their native steelhead from January to March. The farther north one goes, the later in the season the native winter fish arrive.

Not only are native winter steelhead more appealing to the eye than hatchery fish, they have two other qualities that are held in high esteem by steelheaders. Those qualities are size and fight. It's a fact that native steelhead are larger fish on the average than their hatchery clones. The theory is that over the thousands of years since the glaciers receded, only the strongest and largest fish could successfully navigate the many miles of river to spawn. Some rivers are famous for giant, late-winter native steelhead. The Sol Duc, Quinault, Queets and Skagit rivers in Washington are great examples of trophy rivers. All of these rivers have one thing in common, they are all big, brawling, fast-flowing rivers that demand the survival of the fittest.

What it's all about—a lone angler stands knee-deep in 36 degree water in a snowstorm, tied to an unseen force. However, 18 lbs. of fish and a victorious smile can warm the hearts (and hands) of all winter steelheaders.

The same quality that produces size in native steelhead also makes them superior fighters. Not that their size makes them better battlers, it is their tenacity. An eight-pound late winter native could tow an eight-pound hatchery fish upstream. This unbending will and strength to leap falls and navigate rapids can't be duplicated in a pen-raised environment.

A common complaint of winter steelhead anglers (and summertime anglers also) is that hatchery steelhead just do not bite as well as native fish. It's a fact, the majority of native steelhead are ready biters, and are much more aggressive towards a lure. Oregon's Deschutes River is a prime example. Hatchery steelhead there outnumber native fish three to one, yet the angler's catch ratio is three natives to every one hatchery fish. There is a theory for this non-biting behavior in hatchery steelhead. Rivers that receive large hatchery plants usually attract large numbers of steelheaders trying to catch them. This kind of pressure over the years is obviously going to see most of the willing, aggressive biters caught during the run. The fish that survive the gauntlet of sport rods and return to the hatchery are going to be, in the majority, non-biters. This culling is repeated year after year; and after ten years or so, what do you have? A race of predominantly reluctant, non-biting steelhead.

Not that hatchery winter steelhead are totally inferior fish, they provide angling options during a period of the early winter when opportunities to target steelhead would be few. The spoon fisherman has approximately six months of the year to pursue winter steelhead. Whether you go after the last leaves have fallen off the trees in late autumn, or with the new buds of early spring, it would be a long, dreary winter without the cold weather steelhead.

Green Means Go

For those of you that think you are being exposed to some form of driver's education, don't panic. Green is the key river coloration at which spoons can first be effectively fished after a period of high water, a common occurrence with the frequent rains or snow melts of winter. Except for one specific technique, I'll be the first one to tell you to leave the spoons at home when the water has a brown or brownish/green color to it. (See Plunking The Spoon, Chapter 3.) This means there will be less than two feet of visibility. Spoons are not effective in restricted visibility conditions for two reasons.

One, the reason a spoon is so effective in winter is the amount of flash it gives off. In order to achieve the desired degree of flash to attract cold weather steelhead, light must be able to penetrate water. In high, murky conditions, this just does not happen. Two, the spoon is by nature a swift moving lure. You can slow down the presentation to accommodate low visibility conditions (Chapter 3, Driftmending and Backtrolling), but when there is less than two feet of visibility, even when and if a steelhead sees the spoon, by the time the fish moves to take it or tries to follow it, more often than not the fish will lose track of it in the dark water. Leave the brown or brownish/green conditions to the gents with plunking gear.

The best way to gauge if the present river conditions are "spoonable" is to, if possible, wade out into the river up to your knees. If you can clearly see the toe of your boot, you're in business. Any visibility less than that and chances for success are marginal at best.

Green is also the color that means go for traveling steelhead. Winter run fish will begin to move upriver when the water color changes from brown to green. The higher water provides fish with ease of passage upstream. Waterfalls, rapids, and obstructions are cleared with less effort thanks to increased water flows around them. They do not have this luxury in lower water. The green canopy also provides steelhead with a sense of security from predators, and sediment that was present in the higher, brown water is no longer there as an abrasive to their gills. Because steelhead will be moving during periods of dropping, green water, these will be optimum times to fish. When steelhead are moving or have recently moved to a new area they are the most aggressive and willing to strike. That is proven.

While it is true that this condition is the most conductive to success, you should not only fish during these conditions. I know of otherwise talented steelheaders that will only fish during these ideal river levels. There are three viable reasons for not fishing only during "primetime."

Notice the degree of water clarity in the picture. The dark green is the key coloration to look for after a period of high water to start using spoons. This steelhead hit a matte silver/chartreuse BC Steel.

One, when rivers drop into "green," every steelheader in the area code (and their brothers) that have been standing around twiddling their thumbs will be on the river. Unless you like a lot of company, try fishing at other than peak times for a bit more solitude. You will learn faster, and fish with greater efficiency, away from the crowds. Two, you will find that most of the winter season will be spent in a holding pattern waiting for that "just dropped into shape green" condition on your river. Rivers will stay in optimum prime condition for two to three days, tops. A lot of winter steelheading opportunities are wasted by not bothering to fish in other than perfect conditions, which brings up reason number three. Anybody with a fraction of steelheading knowledge (no offense to you beginners) can hook fish when the river is at the "perfect green" stage because steelhead are moving and aggressive. Going out during less than perfect conditions will make you a better steelheader. You will learn how to take fish in lower and slightly higher water, and with a lot less competition. All the "perfect green water" steelheaders will be home complaining about the lack of rain.

Remember, while green means go to the spoon fisherman, it is not the only water color you should restrict fishing outings to. In any sport, there are unfavorable conditions. It is the player that performs well in adverse conditions that is regarded as the best—steelheaders are no exception.

The Myth Of The Novel Alternative

Ask any dyed-in-the-wool drift fisherman why they carry a box of spoons with them in their vest when winter steelheading, and you will receive the same standard answer. They will tell you matter-of-factly that even though their major effort will be plying the river with bait/drift bobbers, there will usually be a time and place where the spoons will come out. That time is late morning, after they have run out of bait, or are now fishing on a stretch of water that has been beaten repeatedly during the morning. The accepted theory is that steelhead will strike a spoon over drift gear in this situation because it is something different, a novel alternative to the myriad of drift gear presented to them all morning. While this may have a ring of truth to it, and it is the most widely accepted theory for a spoon's effectiveness on winter steelhead, it is only half true. That "different look" is not the only reason winter steelhead strike spoons.

This gorgeous native hen took a 5/8th ounce matte silver teardrop spoon in 38 degree water. It came from a stretch of river that had been worked thoroughly (and unsuccessfully) by the morning's parade of bait fishermen.

First is a look at what situations give this theory merit. As discussed in the "Green Means Go" section of this chapter, moving, aggressive steelhead in ideal water conditions will strike almost any kind of steelhead attractor if presented properly. So, theoretically, these willing fish would not let any drift gear go by without striking, therefore the need to switch to spoons would be unnecessary.

This situation changes, however, in periods of extended low water. Fish that are stuck in sections of rivers for many days, even weeks, will become stale to drift gear, especially if there is a lot of pressure on that stream. These steelhead not only have memorized entire catalogs of gear, but have also gotten used to them bouncing by. Consider those small birds you always see on the side of the road, ignoring the cars speeding by no more than a few feet away. This is a conditioned response. The cars pose no threat to the birds, so they are ignored. Steelhead treat the drift gear they see all day long for days on end the same way. A percentage of these fish have probably been stung by bait/ bobbers and relate to their presence by pain. In either situation, drift gear is a losing proposition. The spoon is a novel alternative in these extended low water situations. The steelhead will react aggressively to the spoon in this condition because it is a novel object, something it can't relate to pain or recent memory. This theory has solid reasoning, but there is another reason, one even more important that explains why winter steelhead will strike a spoon.

Consider this example: the winter river you are currently fishing is dropping, has good flow, not optimum "green" conditions, but still contains good numbers of fresh steelhead. You fish a drift with bait/bobber and get nothing, even though you know for certain steelhead are present. You put on a spoon and wham, a fish is hooked. Sounds familiar, doesn't it? The spoon was a novel alternative? No way, these fish are still fairly fresh and have not seen other gear, they are not stranded in one hole for long periods in low water, nor have they been stung. Why did the fish hit the spoon? The answer is the biggest factor in winter steelhead fishing, and that is water temperature.

A typical wintertime river will be between 35 and 48 degrees. That means that steelhead will be, to a degree, lethargic. Unlike their summer run cousins, these cold weather denizens do not live in 54 degree water. While summer fish will be lively and extremely aggressive in the warmer water, winter fish, being in much colder water, won't be. Being less active, winter steelhead will not move or move far for a subtle cluster of eggs, a Corkie, or a fly. Not that they won't take them, they certainly will, but not consistently in the colder water. Consider the earlier example, our fisherman was on a dropping river condition. What causes a drop in winter rivers is normally a lack of rainfall and colder nighttime temperatures, usually below freezing. This means daytime river temperatures will be typically in the mid to upper 30 degree range. Steelhead in these 35 to 40 degree water conditions need a lure that will overcome their lethargy, and excite them into striking. The spoon, being a larger object than most terminal gear, combined with its flash, wakes up the fish and excites them into striking, where other subtle methods won't.

I can verify this by personal experience. Each autumn I fish a large river in British Columbia for exceptional wild summer steelhead. The river conditions this time of year are typically low and clear, with the water temperature varying from 36 to 43 degrees. This is a wintertime condition. The clear water allows you (while traveling up and downstream in a jet boat) to spot steelhead in their lies. Year after year, fishermen have coaxed these fish into striking large silver or nickel plated spoons after fly and/or drift gear fishermen could not get them to respond. Knowing the steelhead were present (by spotting them) proves unquestionably that the spoon's size and flash excited them in the colder water, whereas flies and drift bobbers could not. The colder the water, the greater the frequency this was observed.

Even in periods of prolonged low water, temperature is still a factor. While it may be true a lot of fish in the river are stale, there are always some fresh steelhead moving upstream during the winter run. Remember, low water is caused by colder than normal weather. These low water fish may be new in the river, but due to very cold water temperatures, will not move or move far for a subtle presentation. Here again, the spoon's size and flash will trigger a response from these steelhead. That is why diving plugs and spinners are also lethal weapons in low, cold water. You need a large profile lure with movement and flash to move fish to strike.

So now we understand how spoons can be mistaken as a novel alternative. Keep in mind that spoons do provide the "different look" needed in certain situations, but first and foremost they get steelhead to react in the winter in a way that most methods can't match.

Most Common Mistakes Made By Winter Steelhead Spoon Fishermen

We all know humans are imperfect, and by nature all make mistakes. No one person is infallible, and that fraternity includes winter steelheaders. No matter what technique a person chooses to pursue the cold weather steelhead, he or she should try to avoid making mistakes. Because spoon fishing for winter steelhead is a specialized technique, lack of proper information allows for a great range of river faux pas.

The best way to avoid bad habits is by not making them in the first place. That is what this chapter deals with—pointing out bad habits and mistakes made most often by winter steelhead spoon fishermen.

There is the old steelheader's adage, "the best time to go steelheading is when you can go." For a lot of fishermen, responsibilities to jobs and family leave very little time for their sport. They don't have the luxury of picking the perfect day for winter steelheading. They can still pick days, along with fishermen with a more flexible schedule, when the odds will be in favor of the rodsman. The major mistake made by spoon fisherman, or any steelheader for that matter, is thinking fish will strike in any weather. This is not so, there are definite weather patterns to avoid, they have "skunk" written all over them.

Do not venture out to the river during periods of prolonged, extreme cold. Nighttime lows in the teens and low twenties, and daytime highs of 32 degrees and less, equal river conditions of summer-like low flows and ice forming in the slack water. This means river temperatures that can actually be near freezing (32 degrees or less!). Steelhead in this bitter cold will be more interested in survival than striking, their metabolism lowered so much by the cold that not even the spoon's size and flash can move them to strike. Even when a steelhead can be coaxed to bite, the extremely cold water reduces their fight to that of an old boot with fins. To avoid annoying ice in the rod guides, frigid hands and no fish, stay home and read a good book.

On the flip side, watch out for warm weather fronts that break the grip of cold weather and bring in a lot of rain. A falling barometer means a rainstorm. This will raise water levels, which is desirable, but the combination of a major thaw and a couple inches of rain will cause river levels to jump up much too rapidly. The mistake here is to try and fish during the periods of rising water. The swiftly rising river level forces steelhead to move to slower water, causing the opposite reaction to falling river levels. When steelhead are moved unwillingly, they will totally go off the strike mode. Watch weather patterns closely and avoid these situations like an I.R.S. audit.

Another mistake commonly made is unfortunately perpetuated by most "where to catch steelhead" material. I'm sure you all have read where someone has proclaimed that if a steelhead is caught in a certain spot in a drift, you will always find fish in that spot because each new fish coming upstream will use the same area. This is true, if you fish the river only when it is at one certain level. As river levels change, so do the spots in the holding water where steelhead find cover.

Spawned-out steelhead are easily caught by spoon fishermen. While they still may provide good sport, all ethically mature steelheaders release all downstream fish in hope that they will survive to return next year and spawn again.

A reliable, simple wintertime formula to use is the higher the water level, the lower in the hole and the quieter the water you will find steelhead, and the lower the water level, the higher in the pool they will be. Here is an example. That tailout that you fished with a 1/2 ounce Wob-Lure last week in high, green water held some bright fish. So you come back in a week to find the water has dropped a foot and cleared. You've read where steelhead lie in the same spots, remember? So you pound the tailout and get nothing, while another fisherman walks above you and hits a nice fish on his first cast in the bouncy water at the top of the hole. Ouch!

That tailout held fish in the higher water because, at the present river level, it was the slowest part of the flowing water in the drift and the green color gave the fish a sense of security. At low flow the riffles, deeper water, and bubble curtains at the top of the hole are the only safe place for the steelhead to hide, not in the shallow, clear, slow-moving tailout that has been pounded to a froth.

The only steelhead that can be successfully negotiated from tailouts in low, clear winter water will be spawned out steelhead. Also called "kelts," "spawners," or "fallbacks," these dark, thinned steelhead lie just above the break in tailouts, and are easily caught with spoons. Some may appear nice and bright like a fresh fish, but they are downstream fish that have brightened up, called "mended kelts." You can still identify them by their reddened, inflamed lower fin tips and anal opening, and sunk-in belly. Their white, coarse flesh is worthless for eating, and no amount of smoking or seasoning makes them worth keeping. Please release these downstream travelers in hope that they may return again next year. Real sportsmen do not keep spawners.

Remembering the simple formula for success in changing winter river levels will eliminate the bad habit of fishing the same spot in the drift no matter what the conditions. Completely eliminating mistakes on the river is impossible, even for a seasoned veteran steelheader. Practice and experience will reduce mistakes and will help you keep them at a controllable level.

Matching Spoon Color, Style, And Weight To Wintertime Conditions

This section could very well be an addition to the previous "Most Common Mistakes." Most anglers have the preconception that they only need one style, color and weight of spoon to be fishing effectively during the winter season. I was once a part of that club. I believed that the red/white colors my uncle was so successful with in his heyday were the only ones to use. I also knew that the 1/2 ounce, fat teardrop style

Stee-Lee was the most widely used spoon in Washington, so when I tossed spoons I naturally employed the red/white 1/2-ounce Stee-Lee. And yes, I caught a lot of steelhead with them. But I never made consistent catches. I would have great days and follow them up with dismal ones. I never made the connection until I finally realized (through journal records) that all my steelhead were coming from one specific water height and river location. I was only successful in tailouts during periods of dropping green water with approximately three feet of visibility.

Tailouts were not the only areas I fished. I would watch my partners and other fishermen pull steelhead out from deeper runs consistently with bait/drift bobbers. I would fish the same areas when the tailouts were barren of action, often before the drift fishermen, with a 1/2-ounce fat teardrop and get nil. This was usually followed up by a drift fisherman nailing a fish on his first cast in water I had just pounded. In my early years of steelheading, this was the one occurrence that was the most humbling, frustrating, and maddening I would experience during the winter season. Since I knew my red/white spoons caught steelhead, there had to be a reason for their ineffectiveness. I reasoned that spoons only worked in tailouts. (Give me a break, 18 year olds are not known for rational thought!) Only after experimenting with different styles, colors, and weights of spoons did success finally become regular. After many years, some pretty solid patterns emerged for proper spoon choices in wintertime conditions.

One characteristic that makes spoon fishing enjoyable, as discussed in Chapter 2, is their simplicity. Simple in detail, but you must pay a greater degree of attention when matching spoon weight, style, and color to conditions. You, like I once did, may have a favorite style, weight, and color of spoon that catches the bulk of your steelhead. If you have complete confidence in one style spoon, I'll be the last one to tell you to change. And if you happen to be a beginner, you should stick with one style, weight and color of spoon. However, odds for success can be increased when one becomes willing to change spoons for different river situations. First, we'll look at winter water conditions and which style of spoon works best for each.

When rivers first begin to drop from brownish/green to "spoonable," or two feet of visibility, water flow will be substantial. With the increased flow and dark water, winter steelhead will move to the slower flowing edges of the current. They are not going to fight the heavier currents in the main flow, and the dark green color gives them security. When steelhead are on these edges of the current, which are usually close to the bank, a spoon style that sinks fast is needed. The areas where fish hold in higher water are usually no more than a few feet wide—not much room to allow a lure to sink before it starts to work. Elongated spoons have minimal surface area, so they sink the fastest and therefore are best suited to this type of water. Having a smaller surface area and a more extreme wave in design than other style spoons, they allow for maximum action when worked slowly and vertically. This means the elongated spoon flutters easily even when worked slowly, which is essential when probing the narrow edges in the highest fishable water. Because of the stronger water flows and limited visibility, choose an elongated spoon with a large profile, 3/4 to 1 ounce in weight. In smaller streams with shallower edges, go with a 2/5- to 3/4-ounce spoon.

When rivers drop from "spoonable" green (two feet of visibility) to the "classic" green (3 to 3-1/2 ft. visibility) that every winter steelheader drools over, there will still be considerable flow, but much less than when it was just becoming fishable. This means that the tight edges are now measured in feet, and tailouts become desired target areas. The green hue to the water still provides steelhead with a sense of security, so they will still be in the calmer, shallower water. Since tailouts are characteristically some of the widest, slowest and shallowest areas in rivers, a spoon that does not sink fast is desired to keep from hanging up on bottom in the gentler flow. Here is where the fat, or teardrop style spoon works best.

This style spoon is probably the most common used today for winter steelhead, with the Wob-Lure, Stee-Lee, Kit-A-Mat and Wob-L-Rite the most popular names with the steelheading masses. Why this style of spoon is the most popular escapes me. Perhaps it is because this style is the least expensive on the market, price being the human attractor, not necessarily function. They do

Size of spoon does not necessarily dictate the size of the quarry; spoon choice always depends on present river conditions. The two steelhead pictured came from the same run only days apart, yet were caught on two very different weight, styles, and color/finish spoons. The small bright hen (left) took a 2/5th ounce classic in higher water, and the large buck (right) struck a 1/2 ounce teardrop two days later in the lower flows.

Each river system is unique, so are the native steelhead that inhabit them. These two fish were taken from rivers only twenty miles apart, (in April) yet each fish greatly differs in spawning coloration.

catch steelhead, no doubt, but they are the least effective of all the spoon designs. The reason why makes it clear why these style spoons work so well in tailout conditions, and also explains why I only caught winter steelhead with the red/white Stee-Lees there.

The fat teardrop is the least effective style spoon because unlike any other design, it has the greatest variance in surface area to weight ratio. This characteristic gives the "fat" spoon a tendency to be pushed upward easily, not unlike an airplane wing. This surfacing tendency makes them difficult, if not impossible, to be worked in deep holding water. This does, however, make them desirable for shallow or slow water duty (two to five feet deep), and that includes tailouts. The 1/2- to 5/8-ounce models are the best for these situations. They can also be worked in the now widened, calmer and shallower edges.

When the river drops from "classic" green (3 to 3-1/2 ft. visibility) to six feet of visibility, steelhead behavior changes drastically. The fish no longer feel safe in the shallower water because the green canopy of cover has left, which make the tailouts and edges that hold fish in slightly higher water now void of steelhead. The river does, however, still have a shade of color to it, and it has

a ways to go before reaching low, clear flow. What happens now is the fish have moved to deeper water higher in the pool, preferring the area where bottom is just barely visible to where the whitewater entering the hole stops and starts to flatten out. This is where steelhead find security under these conditions. This is also why a few days after hammering fish in the tailouts with the Stee-Lee I would get skunked fishing the same water.

To target these mid-pool winter steelhead, you need a spoon that sinks moderately fast, can get down but not dig too deep, and still have plenty of action. Under these conditions the oval or classic spoons function best. These style spoons have less surface area, which makes them sink faster, and a greater foil (curvature) that makes them flutter on the sink. The classic, or oval, in 1/2-, 2/5-, 3/4-, and 1-ounce weights will cover all types of this water (four to ten feet deep) adequately.

When winter rivers drop to their final stage (six feet to unlimited visibility), steelhead will again move to find security. With minimal flows and unrestricted visibility, steelhead will be at or near the very top of the hole, where deep and/or broken water is their only cover. The exception is when water temperatures are below 40 degrees. When water temperatures range from 32 to 40 degrees steelhead will also be found in slow, deep water. Spoon style in this situation is a gray area, your choice of spoon technique dictates style. Because the water at the head of the pool is the fastest flowing holding area you will be targeting, a fast sinking spoon like the elongated or the oval is desired. These work fine, but in situations where you can position yourself to back-troll (Chapter 3), a teardrop style may be the choice. Here again, experimentation and experience with different style spoons in low water situations on your river will tell which ones to choose.

Now that spoon size and style has been discussed, the proper color or finish must be determined for levels of visibility. Color may be as large a factor as style. There are literally hundreds of color combinations and finishes commercially available. Ed Eppinger, president of Eppinger Manufacturing, says the reason they sell Dardevles with thousands of combinations of colors is because that is the way fishermen want them. Steelhead, however, do not have much input to tackle manufacturing. Though most of them will catch steelhead, there are only a few color combinations and basic finishes that are needed to take winter steelhead under all spoonable conditions.

When rivers drop to "spoonable," or approximately two feet of visibility, bright colors that stay visible in low light are necessary. Chartreuse, chartreuse/green, chartreuse/black spots, fire orange/chartreuse, or white/chartreuse are the most visible colors in marginal, dark water conditions. Remember, color is normally added only to the convex side of the spoon.

From 2 to 3-1/2 feet of visibility, color is a needed attractor but need not be as bright, because of greater light penetration through the water. Hot pink/white, fire

Brad Bailey photo

orange/matte silver plate, fluorescent red/white, or white/black spots are color enough to get a steelhead's attention. Pattern does not matter in any color. They can be stripes or dots—fish aren't that picky.

From 3-1/2 to 6 feet of visibility, color added to the convex side of the spoon is no longer a necessity. Because the river now only has a slight shade of green, light penetrates easily through all holding water. Now only the brightest natural finishes are needed. By natural I mean metal finishes. White matte silver plate works the best in this condition, because it reflects the most light. Silver is many times brighter than nickel. Nickel under low light or deep water will appear almost black to steelhead. Silver plate reflects brightly in low light, and attracts fish better than any metal finish in cold water. Second choice in this condition is polished copper, or on a sunny day, polished brass.

When there is two to six feet of visibility the white matte silver plate finish is the best all-around choice in the winter, and is the author's favorite. A major problem, believe it or not, is that there are only a few companies that offer spoons in silver plate—and only in a few styles and weights. As of this writing, Luhr Jensen's Krocodile, Gibbs' Koho and Kit-A-Mat, Pen Tac's BC Steel, and Mepps' Syclops are the only silver plated spoons commercially available. Call or write manufacturers for availability of silver plated spoons (see listings in Chapter 1).

Sometimes finding qaulity steelheading close to home is not possible, and travelling the extra miles to find good fishing may be necessary.

This photo proves why silver plating is vastly superior to nickel plating during winter (cold water) conditions. The spoon on the left is plain nickel. Notice how, under bright light conditions, it appears black? The matte silver spoon on the right reflects light, unlike the nickel that absorbs it, making silver 80 percent more visible to steelhead. Silver plating is a key to success under low light/limited visibility conditions.

In the debate over hammered versus plain metal surfaces on the convex side of the spoon, I do not have, nor have found any evidence that one has fish attracting qualities over the other. The theory behind hammered finishes is they reflect more light. By observing both in a side by side test using identical metal finishes, neither seemed to reflect more light than the other. If one surface is better, the difference is insignificant. If you prefer one surface, by all means stick with it.

When there is six feet to unlimited visibility, polished silver plate, plain chrome or nickel work best. Polished silver plate and nickel work well in low, clear winter flows for two important reasons. First is temperature. Remember, the reason a river is low and clear is usually due to a cold snap, which in turn makes the water temperature dip and stay in the 30's. You need the flash of silver plate or nickel to provoke a strike. Second, these finishes give a natural appearance to the spoon, much like a small fish in the same situation. Even when bright wintertime sun pours into the clear water, the polished silver or chrome still attracts well because the water temperature stays low.

You may also be wondering about colored metallic finishes. Blues, greens and the like do not have the light reflecting qualities of natural metal finishes. Again, because of the need for maximum flash to provoke a strike from a cold weather steelhead, the subtle metallic colors will not draw as many strikes. They should be avoided.

Always try to match proper weight, style and color to changing winter water conditions. Now that you have a basis to work with from the guidelines in this section, all that remains is applying it streamside. There is no substitute for knowledge gained by on the river application. I think we can all agree on that.

Chapter 5

Summer Steelhead: The Greatest Reward

For myself and thousands of steelheaders in Washington, Opening Day is a special occasion. You won't find any reference to this date on any calendar. But this is New Year's Eve, the Fourth Of July, and every other holiday rolled into one glorious day. After the traditional spring closure, freedom is almost at hand. Lawns go unmowed. Painting the porch can wait another week. Any other chores? Not today. Opening Day means another season of summer steelheading has begun!

This fever is not exclusive to Washington State, it spreads to wherever sunshine steelhead are found. This is the time of year when fishermen are no longer mummified in five layers of wool. Iced rod guides are replaced with iced tea. Windburn becomes sunburn–get the idea. Not only does summer have the marvelous weather, it has the most dynamic, supercharged steelhead of the year. And summer has been the author's favorite time of year to fish for the last eight years.

It is the summer steelhead that has produced my fondest memories of seasons gone by. How about the August 31st when I watched, slack-jawed, my best friend land his first steelhead. (A 20-pound buck!) That fish repeatedly bolted at full speed into a rock wall until it smashed a good three inches off its snout. There was the October 13th that produced 25- and 26-pound giant bucks on back-to-back casts. The June 20th when my partner set the hook into a silver rocket that shot out of the river and soared two feet over my head. That's right, eight feet straight up. There have even been a couple of unforgettable encounters with Sasquatch. Buy me a beer sometime and I might tell you about it. And finally, I'll never forget the 20-pound-plus steelhead that swam straight up a 15-foot waterfall and broke my 20-pound test line at the top–Seriously!

In this chapter, we'll discuss the summer steelhead's calendar and range, the importance of polarized glasses for summer fishing, how to avoid summertime mistakes, and which spoons and techniques work best (and which do not!) to give you the advantage.

Thousands of steelheaders nationwide worship the summer steelhead. Many chase them because they are the wildest, hardest fighting anadromous fish. Others, like myself, go after them hoping this incredible finned fury will give them one more cherished memory. No matter what it is you expect from a trip to a summer steelhead river, just getting the opportunity to do battle with one is the greatest reward of all.

The Warm Weather Steelhead

Summer steelhead share one similarity with winter fish; they both spawn at approximately the same time in the late winter/early spring– but that is where the similarity ends. Summer run steelhead differ in physical appearance, run timing and in some strains, distance travelled upriver. Unlike their winter-run cousin, they sometimes actively feed.

Summer steelhead enter rivers on the West Coast from as early as February to as late as November, but the bulk of most runs usually occur from May through July. Some rivers get the bulk of their run in June while others may not see the majority of their fish until September. Again, intimately knowing the river that you choose to target summer steelhead in helps immensely when determining peak runs and best fishing times.

Because summer fish can spend up to a year in their home rivers before spawning, their physical appearance

The ultimate gamefish–an early May native summer steelhead, hours out of saltwater, bright as liquid metal.

when first entering freshwater is striking. Because of this duration, summer steelhead are loaded with extra fat, giving them a thicker appearance across the back than a winter fish. Whereas a winter steelhead will look deeper in the belly due to mature egg skeins and milt filling up the body cavity, a fresh summer run will have a leaner look, almost as if it was spawned out. This is due to the fact that eggs and milt are still undeveloped.

While summer and winter fish generally share the same rivers and spawning grounds, there are some runs that differ greatly. These are true summer steelhead, traveling hundreds of miles inland to Eastern Washington, Eastern Oregon, Idaho, and deep into British Columbia. Because of the great distance travelled by these fish, and the time it takes them to get to their destination, they have no competition in spawning areas from winter steelhead. It may take these special fish two to six months to reach their home waters. This rigorous upstream journey has, in a few rivers, produced strains of wild steelhead that are indeed the most impressive in the world for their size, strength and appearance. While it is thought that late-winter, native steelhead are the largest to be had, these system's summer fish are the last truly giant steelhead. The Snake/Clearwater River's "B"

run, and the Skeena system's Kispiox, Babine, Bulkley, Sustut and Copper rivers commonly produce steelhead in the 20-pound range. These magnificent fish deserve our protection and admiration. Other rivers that host runs of long-distance summer steelhead are the Wenatchee, Klickitat, Methow and Grande Ronde in Washington, the Deschutes and John Day in Oregon, and British Columbia's Thompson.

While it is an accepted theory that steelhead do not feed while in freshwater, summer steelhead do. While they will not actively search out food, they will eat if the opportunity presents itself. A recent autopsy of a fresh eight-pound Oregon summer run produced a black pencap! They will "feed" specifically at two different times during their stay in rivers. The first feeding stage is when summer fish first enter fresh water. For the first few weeks the steelhead will feed on anything aquatic or terrestrial it can find. The second stage is late in autumn before winter holdover. One can only speculate why summer steelhead feed during these times, perhaps it is the fish's need for substinance to help tide it over for the duration in freshwater. The steelhead does not need to feed – biologists have proven that. Summer steelhead have all the body fat needed for long stay-overs in rivers.

No other time of the year can the steelheader find such scenic diversity. From the ultra-lush green canopy surrounding the Wynooche River in Washington's rain forest. . .

Wild summer steelhead, at least here in Washington and Oregon, are in the definite minority compared to hatchery fish. Wild fish are also in danger of extinction. In the Columbia River system, 80 percent of the total run of summer steelhead is of hatchery origin. Summer fish (most notably the Skamania strain, produced from crossing Washougal and Wind River native stock) have been planted extensively to literally hundreds of rivers that did not have a fishable number of summer steelhead before, if any at all. Credit must be given to state run departments that have introduced summer steelhead to anglers that would otherwise not have much of an opportunity to catch them in local rivers.

One thought to ponder about releasing hatchery summer steelhead. When water temperatures reach 65 degrees and above, steelhead that are played out have little chance for survival, because oxygen is used up at an accelerated rate in the warmer water. State game officials in Washington, Oregon, and in some Great Lakes areas suggest strongly that all hatchery steelhead caught in warmer water be killed for this reason. Since the fish are of hatchery origin and are planted there to be taken, this is a good idea. Bring a water thermometer and your best judgement.

Hatchery or native, because of their increased body fat, higher metabolism from warmer summertime water temperatures, and because they are actually feeding, summer-run steelhead strike harder with greater frequency, and fight umpteen times better than their winter bretheren. These three factors, plus the fact that a fresh summer run is the brightest thing this side of the Milky Way, is why so many people hold these wonderful fish in such high regard. Whether they are targeted in May or October, it would be tough to imagine a summer gone by without the thunderous charge of a summer steelhead.

. . .to the arid sagebrush of Eastern Oregon's John Day. Just hooking a fish is simply a bonus.

The Blues Brothers

For everyone not familiar with the Blues Brothers, they were a couple of characters dreamed up by former Saturday Night Live cast members Dan Ackroyd and the late John Belushi. Their alter-egos, Elwood and Joliet Jake Blues were, obviously, a couple of white blues singers that did cover versions of old classic blues tunes. What do they have to do with summer steelheading? Their trademark was their polarized Ray Ban sunglasses—they almost never took them off. They would have made great steelheaders because of that. Like the Blues Brothers, you should never be seen on a summer steelhead river without wearing polarized sunglasses.

First and foremost, polarized glasses allow you to see below the water's surface by cutting through the glare. In typical summertime low water conditions, this can have a three point effect. One, the glasses will allow you to spot fish that would go unseen without them. They give the opportunity to fish for these sighted steelhead that normally would be passed by, or accidently spooked. Two, they allow you to see obstructions under the water, such as tackle eating tree limbs, boulders, etc. They will save you money in the long run by not letting you donate spoons to these snags. Three, you will be able to see holding water and pockets that would not be visible without polarized lenses.

Besides allowing you to see underwater, the need for polarized lenses on the river in summer takes on another, more important meaning—a safety meaning. The sun's ultraviolet energy is harmful to the eyes, and the sun's rays reflecting off water can damage eyesight. When fishing for hours in bright sun without the protection of sunglasses, squinting will cause headaches. Long exposure to UV radiation also causes reddening, tearing, rapid blinking, and stinging. Your eyes might feel like they are full of sand, when actually there are hundreds

of tiny ulcers on the outside of the eye. If you are bucking brush to get to a fishing spot, or fishing in a drift boat with other anglers, polarized glasses provide a safety shield from brush or your partner's hooks swung precariously into your face.

When choosing colored lenses, make sure you buy glass instead of plastic. Yellow tinted shades absorb 100 percent of UV radiation and filter out the blue light that also damages eyes. Green and brown tints filter out 99 percent, but cause color distortion. Gray filters out 98 percent, and does not distort colors like brown or green. Gray is the best all-around color; it absorbs UV well and softens all colors equally. However, I have found nothing wrong with the standard brown lenses. Bring a extra pair with you in case you lose or break your originals. Polarized shades are inexpensive; a good pair can be had for under 20 bucks. There are some expensive ones on the market, but they perform no better than the cheaper ones.

Polarized glasses are as important as proper technique and spoon choice on a summer river. Like Jake and Elwood, never be caught without them.

Steelhead so bright, ya gotta wear shades! Avoiding the glare radiating off a newly minted summer run is only one of the many important reasons for wearing polarized glasses on bright days.

Most Common Mistakes Made By Summer Steelhead Spoon Fishermen

When steelheading, more mistakes are made in summertime than during winter. These mistakes are perpetuated by most steelheaders and outdoor writers re-hashing old myths about summer steelhead behavior. And they are just that, myths. Here we will discuss the two main misconceptions that prohibit success on summer steelhead rivers.

One, the fisherman brings a winter attitude and plan of attack with him to the summer river. There is nothing wrong with this theory if you are pursuing long-distance summer steelhead in late fall/early winter. Rivers such as Idaho's Clearwater, Washington's Klickitat, Oregon's Deschutes, and B.C.'s Thompson and Skeena are flowing at wintertime height and temperature that time of year. Even though they are true summer steelhead, they will react to spoons the same way as their winter kin. Steelhead react the same to water temperature regardless of species. But under normal low, warm water summer conditions, looking for steelhead in the same areas in a drift you caught them last winter will get you plenty of casting practice, and not many strikes. This has to do with how steelhead react to summertime water temperatures and clarity.

Since the typical summer river is low and clear for the entire season (with a few exceptions duly noted in the next part of this chapter) and water temperatures will be from 52 to 62 degrees, you will never find steelhead in the deep holes that would have held them last winter. The accepted false belief is that the fish will go deeper to get more cover. This is not so! The deeper water is warmer and has less oxygen in it. The shallowest part of the holding water is where summer steelhead will be found. The head-ins that are bouncy and fast with breaking water, enriching the area with oxygen, and slightly cooler water temperatures is where you will find them. These areas are normally two to four feet deep. The choppy froth at the head-in also gives the steelhead a sense of security it gets no where else in the low, clear water. A steelhead will not strike any lure if it does not feel secure in its surroundings. Anglers that bring their winter mentality to a summer river and pound the deeper areas are going to catch very few fish, even if they are using the proper spoon and color for conditions.

The bright sun of summer will falsely pursuade anglers to fish the deeper, winter-style holding water. The mistake here is the angler believes the bright sunlight drives the steelhead into the deep water to get cover. Again, they will not be there, they will be in the shallowest portion of the holding water at the head-in, lying in the choppy, shallow, highly-oxygenated broken water. But not always. There is a time of day when they will lie in deeper water, from four to seven feet deep with a slight chop on the surface. This sets up the next common mistake.

The second boo-boo is the most common belief preached by anglers that fish for summer steelhead: *the only time of day a summer run will strike is in the first few hours after dawn and again just before sunset.* This concept again comes from the angler bringing a winter steelheading attitude to a summer stream. In the early morning hours and just before sunset, steelhead will move to these deeper areas, due to the subdued light and slightly cooler water temperatures. Fisherman that hit these winter-type spots at the crack of dawn catch fish until the sun hits the water. It is then that the steelhead move up into the shallow riffles. The unknowing steelheader continues to pound the same style water during the mid-day with indifferent luck. From there comes the misconception that summer steelhead hit only at dawn and during evening hours. It's not that the fish won't strike, they just aren't in the same water they were in during the early/late hours. You can see from this how a myth like that could be taken as common knowledge.

Anglers also make the mistake of thinking that even though summer steelhead can be found during mid-day, the bright sun puts them off, and they will not hit anything anyway. How wrong that thinking is, and it amazes me that the majority of the steelheading population buys it. Not only do they strike, but they go absolutely nuts for lures when they are lying in shallow head-ins and riffles. As was discussed in earlier chapters, a steelhead is most aggressive when it has moved to a new location in the pool. Steelhead do not have eyelids, and you would think the bright sun would make them retreat to deeper water to escape it. They don't, they stay shallow. It goes against all logic — a fish being so aggressive in shallow water in bright sunlight, but it's true. They will attack spoons and chase them many feet with a vengeance. Remember to leave a winter steelheading mentality where it belongs, on a winter river.

Salmon Trout Steelheader *editor Nick Amato (left) poses with a Skamania strain summer steelhead. The Skamania summer steelhead is the most widely distributed hatchery fish, planted extensively in Washington/Oregon and all through the Great Lakes. Brad Bailey photo.*

Bright sunlight for long calendar periods can have a negative impact on fishing. When the hot summer sun persists for weeks, raising water temperatures from 65 to 72 degrees, it will put steelhead off. At these extremes fish will cease movement, waiting for cooler water temperatures. Life at 68 degrees for a steelhead means survival. They will rarely strike a lure when water temperatures reach this level. When daytime temperatures get to be 85 to 90-plus degrees for extended periods, stay off the river and wait for a cloudy day or rainfall before returning.

All these mistakes and misconceptions are all made on the low, clear, warmer flows that are typical during the summer months. Remember to concentrate efforts on the head-ins of holes, where the river is fast with a broken surface. Understanding summer steelhead behavior under these conditions will reduce the more common mistakes.

Matching Spoon Color, Style And Weight To Summer-time Conditions

Much of this part of the chapter could be part of the "Most Common Mistakes" made by spoon fishermen on summer steelhead rivers. Just like during winter, most anglers use one style, weight and color of spoon under all conditions and times of day. This section will deal with this habit. To start, we will look at the two types of water conditions found in summer and discuss which spoons work best for each.

The first condition is definitely in minority; rivers that flow colored and cold from snowmelt. As mentioned earlier in this chapter, summer steelhead will gravitate toward the top end of the holding water and lie

When spoon fishing for steelhead in late summer/early fall, a surprise encounter with a sea run cutthroat, coho, or Chinook (posing with the author) is always a possibility.

in the shallow turbulence. This is not the case in rivers that have snowmelt. The reason summer steelhead hold in the head-ins of pools and in shallow riffles is because the water is low, clear, and above 52 degrees. In early summer snowmelt conditions, the air may be very warm, but the rivers will typically be from 42 to 50 degrees. Remember, this is melting snow, not runoff. It is cold! Along with colder water temperatures comes cloudy water from glacier flow, restricting visibility. When dealing with a snowmelt river for summer steelhead, you must revert back to the same formula used when fishing on a winter river. When a river is cold and has less visibility, along with more water volume from melted snow, the summer steelhead will behave and lie in the same areas in the river as their winter relatives.

Use the same spoon styles, colors and weights on an early summer snowmelt river as you would use on a winter river. (See Matching Spoon Color, Style, and Size to Wintertime Conditions in the chapter on Winter

Steelhead.) Given the same water temperature and clarity, summer fish will lie in the exact same water as winter runs. No matter which strain of fish, or time of year they are in the stream, all steelhead react the same to a given water temperature and degree of visibility.

The second most common condition found during the summer and early fall is low and clear water ranging from 52 to 65 degrees in temperature. To show which spoons work best for this condition, we have to break down the river into two times of the day, two sets of water temperatures, and two kinds of weather.

From early morning until the sun hits the water, lighting will be low, and the majority of steelhead will be lying in slightly deeper water from four to seven feet deep with a choppy surface. "Chop" defined here would be anywhere from one-inch high ripples to one foot mini-waves. From dawn to approximately an hour after, a chrome or nickel finish is the best choice, because you still must use a finish that the steelhead can detect in low light. When daylight becomes brighter, from an hour after dawn to when the sun hits the water, change to a polished brass finish to tone down the flash slightly. Anglers that stick with their crack of dawn nickel finish will wind up scaring these high-metabolic fish the rest of the day instead of hooking them. Because the steelhead will be holding in water three to seven feet deep in these early hours, an oval style spoon in 1/2 to 2/5 ounce is the choice for getting down in these mid-depth range situations. From dawn until the sun hits the water, summer rivers are typically 52 to 56 degrees because of the cooling effects of the previous night – not warm enough to put a steelhead off by presenting a solid nickel or brass flashing object. But when the hot sun hits the water, things change quickly!

From late morning (when the sun hits the water) to mid-day, the sun will be pouring maximum light into the river, and steelhead will move into the broken riffles, two to four feet deep. Along with this increased lighting are higher water temperatures, usually from 56 to 62 degrees. This warmer water increases the metabolism of the steelhead to the point where it takes very little flash of the spoon to make it strike. Spoon finish in this ultra-bright condition is extremely important. You want just enough flash to excite the steelhead but not enough to spook it. As a color choice in these wary conditions, dull brass or brass with a black stripe is the choice. Finding a black striped spoon is almost an impossibility, but there is another option.

Purchase some black permanent ink felt-tipped marking pens, and color 1/4 to 3/4 of the convex side of the spoon to cut the flash to a minimum. The "magic marker" is a great trick to make the spoon more subtle without sacrificing spoon size. Re-application is needed from time to time due to spoon contact with rocks and steelhead teeth. It only takes a few swipes with the marker and you are fishing again. Be sure to carry one when on the river so the black ink can be re-applied when necessary.

When steelhead are lying in swift flowing shallow head-ins, the best spoon choice would be one with moderate surface area. Here again, an oval or classic spoon style in 1/4 to 1/2 ounce is the choice. This style sinks well (not as much as the elongated, yet more than the fat teardrop) which allows it to get down fast enough to be presented to fast-water steelhead. The small size of the spoon will not spook fish in bright sunlight. In shallow riffles (two to three feet deep) that do not flow quite as fast as the swift head-ins, a fat teardrop is perfectly suited for the job. Their capacity for greater buoyancy keeps them above the rocks in shallower water. The 1/4- to 1/2-ounce models work best for riffle duty.

When fishing cloudy summer days, steelhead will behave the same after early morning light. They will still move up into the shallow, fast head-ins in clear water. Stick with the same formula for bright days, except when switching to brass spoons for mid-day fishing, the addition of black is not necessary. A plain brass finish works well all day in cloudy situations on low, clear summer rivers.

Following all the forementioned information on matching spoons to summer conditions will hook you up with more summer steelhead, but this is not engraved in stone. I have witnessed (and you may have too) a behavior in summer runs that goes completely against the norm.

This Vancouver Island summer steelhead was lying in two feet of 58 degree glass-clear riffled water. A driftmended 1/4 ounce nickel/black stripe teardrop was the winning combination.

Although they are true summer steelhead, these Babine River natives are fished with winter techniques under cold water/weather conditions.

Given the combination of slightly higher water (slightly higher means anywhere from one to three inches, but still gin clear) and steelhead that have been in the river no longer than a few days, summer steelhead will charge a large, bright lure under sunny conditions. Under these circumstances in the early season when steelhead are moving up to 20 miles a day and are fresh from saltwater they are extremely aggressive, and spoon color does not seem to be as critical a factor. Summer steelhead under these conditions will seemingly smash every color and finish in the catalog. Leave it to the steelhead to make fools out of experts. Since this phenomena only occurs when fish first enter freshwater early in the summer season, for consistent results during the majority of the summer it is best to stick with the earlier mentioned formulas.

Matching proper spoon style, weight and finish is more important in summer than most anglers realize. Once you have practiced and applied knowledge streamside, it will only be a matter of time until your breath is sucked away by the lightning charge of an enraged, chrome bright summer steelhead pouncing on your spoon.

CHAPTER 6

The Tools: Rods, Reels, Line, Hooks, And Swivels

This chapter is necessary because we would all look rather silly standing waist deep in icy water trying to tempt a steelhead to take a hand-held spoon. Seriously, rods, reels, etc., are the tools to build up steelheading skills.

Too many anglers either sell themselves short or depend too much on their outfits. While I'm not going to tell you to use a specific outfit, there are some that definitely make spoon fishing easier and more effective. No preaching about brand-name rods, reels, lines or hooks. Why? Every time you are out on the river, how many steelheaders do you see using the same outfit? Right. Each individual is different, and so is their taste in gear. All we are going to look at is which ones will make spoon fishing for steelhead the most practical.

Rods: The Important Match

Matching spoon weight to rod strength is the key to this part of the chapter. As was stated earlier, each fisherman has a different idea about what the "best" outfit consists of. So the debate of ultra high modulus composites vs. graphite, graphite vs. glass, etc., is moot. It's not what the rod is made of that creates a proper match, but the strength of the blank that is all important.

Every commercially made steelhead rod blank has a recommended lure weight inscribed just above where the front cork grip would be placed. This tells the maximum weight of spoon the blank can handle without taxing its strength by over-flexing. For example, a rod with a line test recommendation of 10- to 20-pound test will have a lure weight recommendation of 1/2 to 1-1/2 ounces. This means that the blank will throw a spoon weighing up to 1-1/2 ounces without over-flexing. Over-flexing equates to lost control both on the cast and while working the lure. The most important thing to remember when selecting a rod is to choose one that can handle the weight of the lure you intend to use.

All commercially manufactured rods have a lure/line weight rating on this part of the blank.

When choosing a rod for river spoon fishing, never pick a blank that is too light for the weight of spoon to be used. This 10 to 20 lb. line weight rod cast a 2/5th ounce with satisfying results.

On the flip side, using too heavy a blank with too light a spoon will hamper accuracy and distance when casting. Without enough flex in the rod, you must contort and twist your body on the back cast to achieve necessary rod speed to throw the spoon any distance. A heavy blank will not load up enough with a lighter spoon than recommended for use. This extra exertion will be a fatigue factor after a full day's worth of casting.

Another reason to avoid using too light a blank is hooksetting ability. An example is if a blank is rated up to 1-1/2 ounces and you are throwing a one-ounce spoon, there will be enough backbone to drive the hook home with the larger hook on the bigger lure. Too much flex in the blank makes it difficult to get a proper hook set.

It would be clumsy trying to cast a 3/4-ounce spoon on an ultralight blank rated for four- to eight-pound test and 1/16- to 3/8-ounce lures. The rod would also max out in an ineffective full bend when on tried to get a good hook set. Using too light a rod for the lure will cause the rod to load up in a deep "C" bend, and very little force will be transferred to the lure to push the hook home. Light blanks are fine for drifting bait with fine hooks, or tossing small spinners, but are not practical for spoon fishing. Remember, you may go with more backbone, as strong of a blank that suits an individual's taste and still have an effective spoon rod, but going lighter will give up hooksetting power with larger spoons and hooks.

Rod length is also a matter of personal preference, but there are a few advantages to using a longer rod when spoon fishing. The typical steelhead rod is 8-1/2 feet long. This is the minimum recommended length for spoon fishing, and the majority of fishermen are comfortable with this length. However, a rod of 9 to 9-1/2 feet allows more line to be held out of the water on a presentation. What the longer rod does is allow you to work the spoon slower and deeper because of less line drag. Line drag speeds up the drift consequently making the spoon lift upwards.

Reels: A Matter Of Choice

It's a fact that the majority of steelhead fishermen use level-wind reels. It seems to be a given that when an angler reaches a certain skill level, they must use a level-wind reel. This being a direct result of peer pressure. Anyone seen going after steelhead with a spinning reel is chuckled at under the breath and is automatically labeled a beginner, or one severely lacking in skill. That statement is a fallacy, brought on by lesser skilled steelheaders mocking what they do not understand. The following states how each type of reel has advantages and disadvantages which result in trade-offs in effectiveness.

Level-wind reels can be cast as far as open face spinning reels, but can suffer from backlashes. The spinning reel is almost foul-proof. Level-winds have better drag systems because the line comes off the spool in a straight line instead of a sharp angle off the bail of a spinning reel, which increases friction on the line and adds to drag pressure. Level-winds cannot be used effectively in tight, brushy quarters where there is no room for a back cast. Spinning reels can be cast effectively from any position. Line can be fed with greater ease and control from a level-wind to extend drifts or to allow a lure to keep in contact with bottom; it is almost impossible to do the same with a spinning reel.

You can see from this list of pros and cons that each style of reel has advantages and disadvantages.

When buying a new reel, there are a few design features to look for. Select spinning reels with a front drag, on top of the spool. These drag systems are superior to rear control drags. Although not as readily accessible, these front drags have larger discs and can take the punishing runs of a large fish over a season better than the smaller disc rear drags.

Look for simplicity in level-wind reels. All the bells and whistles, control panels, aerodynamic fins, and rippin'-pitchin'-flippin'-spittin' options are unnecessary accessories that do nothing but get the attention of the buyer (usually a bass fisherman) and can be one more thing to go wrong and jam up the reel when a steelhead goes berserk. All these useless gadgets on the reel reduce the width of the spool, restricting the amount of line capacity that may be desperately needed with a hot fish.

I personally prefer a level-wind for spoon fishing in rivers, because throwing a concentrated weight like a spoon makes casting the level-wind easy, and I'm able to pay out line quickly to stay in constant proximity of the bottom. But I will be the last person to tell another to switch if the angler is comfortable and successful with their favorite style of reel.

Reels are truly a matter of personal choice. These out of production Shimano 200 series level-wind offered simplicity with perfect function, and are the author's all time favorites.

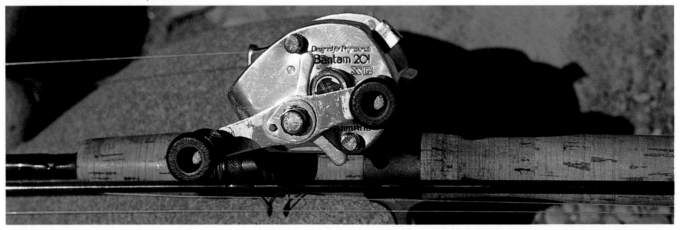

Lines:
The Critical Connection

When selecting monofilament lines for spoon fishing, line diameter must be considered for five important reasons. Surprisingly, none of them have anything to do with the thickness of the mono putting off the fish from biting. When a steelhead bears down on a spoon (or any other lure like a diving plug or spinner) its attention is focused exclusively on the movement of the object, and it is oblivious to the presence of any line attached to the lure. Therefore, using heavy lines like 15- to 20-pound test will not, even in clear water, cause a significant reduction in strikes. I know of perhaps a dozen steelheaders that back-troll plugs and fish spinners with heavy monos, regardless of water clarity, and do very well.

Your first consideration for line diameter is hooksetting ability. When using spoons with larger hooks, it takes a bit more power to drive the wider hook point into the steelhead's bony mouth. Let me give some examples. If you were using a 3/4-ounce spoon with a No. 3/0 Siwash hook, any line testing less than 10- pound test would more than likely break after applying the required power for a proper hook set. The same 10-pound test, however, would be fine when using a 1/4-ounce spoon with a No. 1 Siwash hook. The smaller hook is thinner in diameter and requires less power to drive the point home. For spoons, never use lines testing less than 10-pound test, even for the smallest spoons. The force that a steelhead strikes the spoon is strong enough to instantly snap any lighter test line, especially if the angler is not prepared for the take. (See chart for matching line test to spoon and hook size.)

When fishing spoons in river systems notorious for trophy sized steelhead, heavy pound test monofilament is mandatory. Fact: using heavier lines will not cause a reduction in strikes.

The second consideration is the size of steelhead targeted. If you are fishing rivers where there are exceptional fish to be had, such as California's Smith, Washington's Quinault and Skagit, or any of the mighty Skeena River tributaries in British Columbia, line diameter should be beefed up accordingly. Fifteen- to 20-pound test lines are the norm for spoon fishing these rivers. A trophy of a lifetime could be lost due to too light a line. Remember, you will not suffer a reduction of strikes by using a heavier line, so give yourself the advantage of strong monofilament when targeting larger fish.

Third, you must consider the catch and release factor. Using a heavier pound test will allow steelhead to be landed faster thereby not exhausting the fish and allowing lactic acid to build up in its muscle tissue. The sooner a steelhead is landed that you intend to release, the greater chance it has to fully recover and continue on to spawn.

Your fourth consideration is loss of lures. When using heavy mono, most spoons can be retrieved by applying the strength of the line to pull the spoon free. In many instances, if the hook is snagged it will bend out until it no longer grabs the rock or tree limb. Replacing a bent hook is less expensive than replacing a spoon.

Using heavy test monofilament will let you set the hook easier, control large fish, allow steelhead to be landed faster for better survival after release, and allow you to retrieve more spoons from snags, all without causing a reduction of strikes. The fifth and last consideration is the only disadvantage to the use of heavier pound test when spoon fishing in rivers. Heavy lines will cause greater water resistance. This means spoons will not sink as quickly as with lighter test, and they cannot be worked as slow. The tradeoff is slight in comparison to the plus factors heavier monofilaments have over thinner diameter lines.

In the debate over fluorescent lines vs. monos that reflect natural colors (such as greens and browns), there are a few points to ponder. First it is unquestionably important to be able to watch your line during the entire presentation. Not knowing what angle your line is at or its location in the drift results in a lot of water not being covered or worked properly. Natural colored lines are almost impossible to follow visually through a drift, because they blend in so well with the background. Not seeing the line will cost you fish, and not knowing exactly where the spoon is will cost money in lost gear to snags. This is not a pitch to use a fluorescent line, they can be obscenely bright when fishing in gin-clear water for skittish summer runs, which is probably the only condition where line color can directly affect the number of possible strikes. A good trade-off is to use a clear or soft, eye-ease tone line. You will still be able to follow the path of the spoon throughout the drift without resorting to neon monos.

Remember when choosing a monofilament line, you get exactly what you pay for. We all fork over a lot of paper Presidential portraits for top of the line gear. It doesn't make sense to spend all that money and then settle for a cheap line that will lose more lures and fish than it will bring in. Premium monos are more expensive for many good reasons! They are abrasion resistant, have superior knot strength, are uniform in diameter, absorb shock better and last a lot longer. Sure, it's great getting a thousand yards of line for a buck and a half, but how great is it going to feel after breaking off the steelhead of a lifetime because of poor knot strength, thin spots in the mono and general brittleness? Line is so very important – get the best you can possibly afford.

Hooks: The Great Debate

Want to start an argument? Get a hundred steelheaders in a room and ask them if they prefer single or treble hooks attached to their lures. Again, here as in other aspects of personal equipment, each fisherman has their own reasons for using singles over trebles and vice versa. While this may be fuel for a debate, I will try to provide a realistic point of view toward which style of hook is superior to the other.

There are two styles of hooks you should use for spoon fishing: singles and trebles. If the choice is a single hook, use the best quality Siwash style. The Siwash has a longer point than a regular style bait hook, and a rounder, truer bend. The large eye allows the hook to move freely on the split ring, and the open eye allows for a faster hook change. You can simply drop on another and pinch the eye shut with pliers. The Siwash is not pre-offset bent, so they should be bent in an offset position to increase hooksetting ability.

If the choice is treble hooks, go with the highest quality round bend trebles. The round bend trebles are stronger than other styles of treble hooks, because the pull of a hooked fish is distributed evenly on the bend, and not in one spot on the bottom of the hook. It is a stronger designed treble.

When making the choice of which style of hook to use (single or treble), please consider the following observations. If a comparable size treble and a single Siwash hook are placed side by side, one thing is noticed immediately. Each individual hook on the treble, compared to the single, is not nearly as large. These smaller hooks will cause many a steelhead to come loose soon after the strike, due to the fact that unless one of the hooks really finds bone, there is not much hook to hold an acrobatic fish for long. The single Siwash, being a much wider hook in the gap than the treble's smaller hooks, will grab more of the steelhead's mouth, and this will result in a better hold.

It is also much harder to set a treble hook than a single. Think about it, what would require the most power to push into the hard, bony plates of a steelhead's mouth, three hooks or one? Right. I'll bet that all of you have removed treble hooks from steelhead that were bent and twisted beyond further use because of the fish's jaw pressure. There is no jaw pressure on a single hook. That means less hooks to be replaced, and that is cheaper in the long run. Also note that single Siwash hooks are less expensive than trebles.

Steelhead can also use the extra hooks on trebles to pry the one(s) imbedded in their mouth loose. I have observed (and lost!) steelhead, especially large bucks, trying to bury their heads in rocks and underwater foliage attempting to rid themselves of the hook. Many times the exposed hook(s) on the treble will snag the underwater object and allow the fish (using leverage) to rip itself free. With a single hook, this is impossible. I have also observed all too many times a good fish come off at the net because an exposed hook from the treble caught in the mesh, just as the head of the steelie was sliding into the basket.

You probably sense that I prefer single Siwash hooks over trebles on spoons. There are two other reasons that I use singles instead of trebles. First, single hooks allow a spoon to have a more natural action because of less water resistance. And second, by using single hooks you are always fishing legally. Many rivers today have laws that require the use of single hooks on non-buoyant lures. You are always ready to fish without having to switch from trebles to singles.

When using single hooks on spoons, positioning the hook so the point faces the concave side greatly increases your chances for a hookup on the strike.

The area between the dotted line and hook point/spoon body equals "bite" area – notice how much more area "B" has than "A."

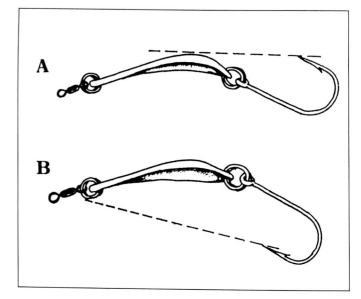

As the spoon moves through the water, figure that water pressure will hold the hook in a straight back position 80 percent of the time it is in motion. Given the shape of the spoon body, it is easy to see where there is more "bite" area in figure "B" than "A." The convex side, having a "hump," deflects the spoon body away from the steelhead's mouth on the strike.

In figure "A," you can see where even the slightest deflection can push the hook point away from the "bite" area. In contrast, when a fish grabs a spoon with the hook in the "B" position, there is no "hump" to deflect the spoon, just increased "bite" area. Whereas in "A," the bite area is from the top of the convex hump near the base of the spoon to the hook point; in "B" it extends from the head of the spoon just below the swivel/split ring to the hook point. This means "B" has 75 percent more area to solidly hook a fish than "A".

Regardless of whether you prefer trebles or singles, it is important to match hook size to spoon size. (See chart that matches line, spoon, and hook size.) Too large a hook, single or treble, will ruin the action of a small spoon in the 1/4- to 1/2- ounce sizes. This is because the increased force of water on the large hook would overwhelm the action of the smaller spoon. Of course this can be said for any hook that is too large for the spoon body. On the flip side, too small a hook on a larger spoon would not inhibit its action, but because heavier gear is used with larger spoons, the risk of a straightened hook is greater.

Another tip that will make setting the hook easier is to pinch down the barb(s) on the hook(s) halfway down. By doing this you have reduced the barb's width by one half, making for easier penetration into the hard mouth of a steelhead. By pinching the barb halfway, enough barb is left to hold a thrashing fish, yet there is less to remove, allowing for an easier release. A narrower barb also causes less damage to a steelhead's mouth.

It doesn't matter if you are a faithful user of trebles or singles, always buy the best single Siwash and round bend trebles you can afford. The anguish of a lost steelhead makes the few cents you saved on hooks a bitter pill to swallow.

CHART FOR MATCHING SPOON STYLE AND SIZE TO HOOK(S), AND RECOMMENDED LINE TEST

Spoon Style	Spoon Size	Hook Size Single	Treble	Line No. Test
Fat Teardrop	1/4 Ounce	No.2 - No. 1	No. 6	10 - 12 lb.
	1/2 Ounce	No. 1/0 - No. 2/0	No. 4	12 - 15 lb.
	5/8 Ounce	No. 2/0	No. 4	12 - 20 lb.
Oval and Classic	1/4 Ounce	No. 2 - No. 1	No. 6	10 -12 lb.
	1/3 Ounce	No. 1	No. 6	12 - 15 lb.
	2/5 Ounce	No. 1/0 - No. 2/0	No. 4	12 - 20 lb.
	3/4 Ounce	No. 2/0 - No. 3/0	No. 4 - No. 2	15 - 20 lb.
	1 Ounce	No. 3	No. 4 - No. 2	15 - 20 lb.
Elongated	1/4 Ounce	No. 1	No. 6	10 - 12 lb.
	1/2 Ounce	No. 1 - No. 1/0	No. 4	12 - 15 lb.
	3/4 Ounce	No. 1/0 - No. 2/0	No. 4	15 - 20 lb.
	1 Ounce	No. 2/0 - No. 3/0	No. 4 - No. 2	15 - 20 lb.
Thin Blade or Plunking Style	No. 1, 1/8 Ounce	No. 1 single Siwash		10 - 12 lb.
	No. 2, 3/16 Ounce	No. 1/0 - No. 2/0 single Siwash		12 - 15 lb.

Swivels And How To Make
The Best

The importance of adding a swivel to the spoon goes without saying. Line twist is inevitable, especially when fishing a revolving lure like a spoon. Even though spoons should wobble and not spin to be at their peak effectiveness, spoon spin is inevitable. To fish a spoon without the addition of a swivel would be unthinkable.

There are two practical choices for hooks on spoons—singles (as shown) and trebles. Each type has plus and minus factors that bring out an angler's praise or disdain.

The number one problem resulting from spoon spin is, obviously, line twist. Twisted line makes casting difficult and severely weakens the monofilament by causing damaging kinks throughout. A swivel not only prevents line twist, it allows the spoon to work uninhibited, away from the line. In other words, the spoon does not have as much action when restricted to a direct connection to the line. Also note that most spoons have a relatively sharp edge around the hole at the head of the body. This sharp edge will greatly weaken any knot. A rounded swivel eye is the proper place to tie a knot.

Okay, you say, the swivel is very important. Which ones do I use? I can recommend two specific setups for swivels on spoons. Neither one resembles the cheap, weak brass snap style that can be purchased a hundred for a buck. You make both of these swivel connections at home.

For the first one, start with an 11/16 inch (between 1/2 and 3/4 inch) No. 3 Duo-Lock style snap. These are the same size snap connectors you will find on the lip of the No. 30 Hot Shot diving plug. Unlock both sides of the snap and add a No. 7, crane/barrel-type swivel. This is a very strong snap swivel that has two distinct advantages, besides its strength. One, the rounded end of the snap allows the spoon to work uninhibited by any right angle bends other style snap swivels may have. Two, by simply unlocking the snap you may change spoons in seconds—no knot to re-tie. This style of snap swivel may also be purchased through several mail-order catalogs. (See listings in Chapter 1.)

The second style of swivel does not give the advantage of quick change, but is perhaps stronger. Simply attach a No. 4 or 5 round split ring to the hole at the head of the spoon, and then add the No. 7 crane/barrel swivel to the split ring. Be sure to use a round split ring because the oval styles have a tendency to twist and/or straighten under the pressure of a large steelhead.

Whichever swivel setup you choose for spoon duty, snap or split ring, you will not be disappointed by their effectiveness.

Alan Burr holds his first spoon-caught steelhead. This fish was hooked on a Little Cleo.

Chapter 7

The Road To Becoming A Successful (Spoon) Fisherman

In essence, this chapter is the bond that solidifies all the content from the other chapters, much like cement in a brick wall. However, very little material here will specifically deal with spoon fishing directly; it will concentrate more on the important principles of steelheading. Without applying these principles on each trip to the river, becoming a respected practitioner of any steelheading technique is impossible. Today, more so than ever, angling ethics are as important as technique.

And yes, this part of the book is directed to a degree toward the inexperienced steelheader. The intentions are to insure that their first steps are taken in the right direction. Even the experienced veteran should be able to pick up some useful bits of information.

The road to becoming a successful spoon fisherman is a long one—a road that has no dead end. Every steelheader who chooses to better himself, beginner or veteran, never stops accumulating knowledge. In this chapter we will look at ideas and principles that can make you a better fisherman. Ideas that will produce more fish and, most importantly; ideas that will produce steelheaders held in high regard by others.

Experience, Persistence, Confidence, and Fine Tuning

"As no man is born an artist, so no man is born an angler."
– Izaak Walton
from *The Complete Angler,* **1653**

What Sir Izaak Walton said in his angling classic rings as true today as it did back then—even more so when applied to today's steelheader. In each previous chapter I have stated that no matter what has been taught in this text, it does not amount to anything unless it is applied streamside.

Experience has many faces; the most familiar is time. To help illustrate how time is relevent to experience, let's look at the world of professional football. Take, for example, the greatest quarterback of all time, Joe Montana. (Let it be known that I am one of the 49er Faithfuls, so please hear me out.) He did not just step onto the field at Notre Dame and start throwing touchdowns. It took many years of practice before he was picking apart NFL defenses. Steelheading, regardless of chosen technique, is no different. Nobody just picks up a rod and is magically transformed into a steelheader. Even with an experienced mentor showing the way there is still the time element. With every minute put on the stream bank knowledge gains interest. Mr. Montana learned, with time, how to be successful when up against a certain defense. You, with time, will recognize which spoon techniques will be successful under different river conditions. There is no shortcut.

Remember to always ask permission first before crossing any posted or private lands that access a river. This fisherman seems to have difficulty reading English, a common malady among steelheaders!

Experience comes from time on the water combined with two important virtues. The first is unyielding persistence. The time spent learning on the river is always accompanied by a certain amount of frustration. Learning any technique, such as spoon fishing in rivers for steelhead, requires untold hours of matching technique to conditions. This process is hard work; much of the time is spent just getting familiarized with the mechanics and reading water, not playing fish. All this "down time" is naturally frustrating. Persistence in believing that your tactics are correct for the conditions will get you through the frustrating times. The result will eventually be increased hookups. This may sound crazy, but sticking with your chosen spoon technique until you are consistently successful with it will be even more gratifying than actually playing the steelhead. True expertise can only be obtained by the angler's persistence in overcoming learning obstacles.

Matched with persistence is the other important virtue of experience, total confidence. Questioning the accepted highest level of any technique is right, because raising any steelheading technique to a new level of effectiveness is always a possibility. All great steelheaders seem to raise their skills to another level. They have done this with an unwaivering belief that they are fishing in the most effective way. The same confidence should be brought with you to the river. If you believe that you are not fishing effectively or that no steelhead will be caught then neither will happen. Having confidence in your chosen technique is as important as the technique itself. Without total confidence, you will not have the mental or physical discipline to use a chosen method to its optimum effectiveness. Simply believing that you will catch steelhead gives the needed edge over other anglers that have even minor doubts about their chances of success. They will not be fishing with the same intensity, cast after cast, as the steelheader that has complete confidence fish will be hooked.

As stated earlier in this chapter, the road to becoming a successful spoon fisherman never ends; there is always room for improvement – to learn more. Even the angler that has many years of experience, unyielding persistence and total confidence under his belt can always fine tune techniques. Fine tuning means not only practicing the technique of choice to perfection, but also leaving yourself open to new ideas. Without an open mind and a willingness to listen to and learn new ideas, no room for growth is left. Too many talented steelheaders are complacent and stubbornly satisfied with the level of expertise they are at. Great steelheaders are never satisfied. They never stop fine tuning, listening, reading and observing. Anglers that refuse to accept new ideas are usually slaves to a certain style of fishing they are occasionally successful with. And they will often vocalize their objections when suggestions are made to change. Remember, knowledge never enters the head through an open mouth. These

To gain experience, go fishing as often as possible, and under all kinds of conditions. As the author found out even blizzards can be productive.

fishermen that refuse to fine tune themselves will be stuck halfway up the ladder of success. Always be willing to read or listen to other angler's ideas, no matter what their level of skill. They may be on to something you have never observed or heard of before. By fine tuning you will constantly improve as a steelheader.

There are some informative books on steelheading available from Frank Amato Publications that can be invaluable to you. They do not deal with spoon fishing directly, but the author's observances on steelhead behavior is gospel. They are *Dry Line Steelhead and Other Subjects* by Bill McMillan, *Spinner Fishing For Steelhead, Salmon and Trout* by Jed Davis, *Greased Line Fishing For Salmon (And Steelhead)* by Jock Scott, *Western Steelhead Fishing Guide* by Milt Keiser, and, though a bit outdated, *Steelhead Drift Fishing* by Bill Luch. These great angler's years of research will help you immensely.

Persistence in believing your chosen technique is the correct one for current conditions will keep you fishing with confidence. It will pay off with strikes, perhaps from a trophy sized fish like this one.

This is the best way I have found to hook more steelhead— go fishing with someone that has more experience than yourself and fish behind them all day!! Watch their every move. Mimic their technique and experience how it feels to fish that particular piece of water the same way.

Do not fish in front of these teachers. Sure, you may hook a steelhead before them, which strokes the ego, but you will be the loser in the long run. By fishing first you will also be showing off inferior skills to a better fishermen. Instant gratification of outfishing a superior steelheader will guarantee a lost chance at on-the-stream tutoring. Swelled heads usually represent shrunken expertise.

In this book I have done my best to tell everything I know about spoon fishing for steelhead. But, unless you take this information and use it in combination with on the river experience, have complete confidence in the techniques and are persistent with them, success will not come. I can't emphasize enough that there is no substitute for hard work streamside. It is the only way.

Keeping A Journal

Most steelheaders believe that the only valuable information comes from successful days on the river—not so! Fishless days can tell you as much, or in many cases, even more about steelhead behavior than days when you score. Everything that occurs while on the water is important to future achievements. Any and all information about date, water temperature, water clarity, weather, style of spoon, etc., can be lost if you rely entirely on memory. Over the years, untold amounts of information could be saved by taking a few minutes after each trip and entering the day's events in a journal.

Enough can't be said about the importance of keeping a journal. I rely on mine as a reference to every aspect of steelheading. Over the years, you will see patterns develop in run timing, steelhead behavior, best lures for conditions—little things that would have been lost if trusted to memory. I plan all steelheading trips by past entries—when chances for success will be the best. The journal rarely lets me down. After a few years of keeping records, definite patterns will emerge that should have a huge effect on your future steelheading ventures.

Date: _____ Time: _____   ☐ Steelhead _____
                                                ☐ Salmon _____
Lake/Stream: _____ ☐ Trout _____
Location/Pool: _____ ☐ Other _____

Water Conditions –
Temp.	☐ 33-39	☐ 40-43	☐ 44-49	☐ 50-53
	☐ 54-57	☐ 58-62	☐ 63-67	☐ 68 + ___
Clarity	☐ 0-2 ft.	☐ 2-6 ft.	☐ 6 ft. +	
Surface	☐ Smooth	☐ Lt. Brkn	☐ Hvy. Brkn	
Depth	☐ 0-4 ft.	☐ 4-8 ft.	☐ 8-12 ft.	☐ 12 ft. +__
Speed	☐ Slow	☐ Medium	☐ Fast	

Water Type –
☐ Head	☐ Fast
☐ Run	☐ Pocket
☐ Tail	☐ Riffle
☐ Rapid	☐ Break
☐ Other _____

Lighting/Weather
Sunlight
☐ Bright/Direct
☐ Indirect
☐ Shade
☐ Light Clouds
☐ Heavy Clouds
☐ Wind

Weather Notes: _____
_____
_____
_____
_____
_____

Lure/Presentation
Lure: _____

Presentation –
☐ Upstream	☐ Downstream
☐ Across	☐ Bottom
☐ Mid-depth	☐ Surface

The first key to having a complete journal is to go into as much detail as possible. This involves a lot of writing, but every little bit entered is valuable future information. Remember to write down everything that happened. Even the smallest detail. The following chart was put together by David Kilhefner, a native Oregonian and skilled angler. It can be carried on your person in a pocket or vest for immediate on-the-river recording.

This chart can then be transferred to a more detailed journal at home. You will be thankful for the journal's valuable information over the years. It can also be a great source of entertainment. On days when you can't be on the water it makes for some wonderfully nostalgic reading.

Out of the countless steelheading trips I have made, most of them would be lost in time without the aid of my journal to jolt my memory. I don't ever want to forget those days—the good and the bad, the friends I shared them with, the special rivers, and the magnificent steelhead caught and lost. Most importantly, I owe most of my steelheading expertise, and the majority of what you are reading in this book, to journal information. Keeping a precise, detailed journal is your vehicle to ride down the road to becoming a successful spoon fisherman.

Avoiding The Lemming Syndrome

The lemming is an animal that is recognized by one very bizarre feature in its behavior. Every year during their migration period some groups will, one after another by the hundreds, jump into bodies of water and subsequently drown after exhaustion takes over. Even though death is inevitable, they will still follow one another into the water. This is just one example of the many unexplained occurrences in nature. Humans, most noteably the steelheader, often display the same quirks in behavior. These actions can be explained, however. Like lemmings, steelhead fishermen "follow the leader" to popular areas. When trying to become a knowledgeable steelheader, following the crowds will be a personal "drowning."

Most anglers, especially ones with limited steelheading experience, are usually drawn to areas they figure will give them the greatest chance to catch a fish. This is done by reading the outdoor blurbs from daily local newspapers, researching catch statistics from previous years, and weekly fishing report tabloids. This journalistic dribble draws crowds to hatchery fish stacking areas. The inexperienced steelheader, after reading about all the fish being caught in these spots, naturally makes a bee line to them. Remember, in a spot where large numbers of fish are being taken, an even larger number of anglers are there trying to catch them. Areas where there are crowds of steelheaders are never good areas to learn how spoon fish.

As a spoon fisherman, you will encounter situations on today's busy rivers when "spoon etiquette" must be practiced. Each steelheading technique is carried out at a different speed through holding water. Spoons can be one of the faster presented techniques. Therefore, you will be using a swifter moving lure than the drift fishermen around you. This disrupts casting timing in the "line-up," producing more tangles and bad feelings with your bankmates than you will want to deal with. Stay away from drift gear tossers, plunkers, and fly fishermen and fish with other spoon anglers, or stay by yourself on an uncrowded piece of water.

The price to be paid for following everyone else (like a lemming) to these popular spots is two-fold. In a crowded situation, competitiveness will overshadow sportsman-like ethics every time—human nature rearing its ugly head. Besides discourtesy, the steelheader will find hot, short tempers, tangled lines, noise unassociated with the outdoor experience, litter, and 100 percent of all landed fish will be unceremoniously drug in and killed—every one. This type of media-induced frenzy produces a tarnished view of steelheading that is almost criminal and not one bit enjoyable. Under these circumstances with this type of pressure, there is no way to effectively practice and apply spoon techniques, or any steelheading technique for that matter. Avoid these situations, no matter how tempting fishing like this may seem to be.

Steelhead that are subjected to this hammering pressure do not react in a natural way. Fish that have been pummeled by drift boats, jet sleds and bank traffic will not be "relaxed" in their environment, especially in

Staying away from crowds will allow you to properly practice techniques, and present the spoon to undisturbed steelhead. Nick Amato uses this 10 foot mini-drifter to do just that on uncrowded Oregon coastal rivers.

low, clear water situations. No technique works when fish have been subjected to constant harassment by repeated casting and boat/foot traffic. Find a stream free from crowds where you can have some lonely water to work. They are out there, believe me, even in this day when it seems like there are so many fishermen it is almost impossible to find solitude. All it takes is a little research and exploration. The only way to do anything properly when steelheading is to do it yourself, and that includes finding a river to practice on. This could mean driving a few extra miles or walking a bit farther off the beaten path. Extra effort will pay off in undisturbed steelhead that will react naturally when presented with the right technique for conditions.

The gist of this is to avoid being trapped in the "lemming" attitude that permeates the minds of so many steelheaders today. I realize that finding solitude is sometimes not possible, due to time, monetary and geographic limitations for some anglers. I do, however, firmly believe that putting in some extra time and effort will enable you to find spots, even on a busy river, that will allow knowledge to be applied streamside as it was intended—away from the crowds.

The Importance Of Catch And Release

*"I submit first of all there is no such thing
as sport without ethics."*
— Roderick Haig-Brown, 1966

No matter how much experience and knowledge one possesses, without ethics, you cannot become a successful spoon fisherman. Now more than ever, principles must be practiced and taught by all if river fishing for steelhead has a chance for a bright future.

Wild, free-flowing rivers and the priceless steelhead that live in them—their future is in our hands.

Most outdoor writers paint a wonderful, exciting, rosy picture of the present state of their sport—it sells. I'm not going to do that. The number of West Coast steelheaders (and I suppose Great Lakes areas also) are growing exponentially every year. With more fishermen comes the demand for more steelhead. Along with this demand is the horrible conditions of wild strains of steelhead. They are disappearing by the ways of antique game laws that do not require mandatory release. British Columbia seems to be the only area concerned about preserving native runs. The majority of the province requires the release of all wild steelhead.

Add to these problems pollution, destruction of spawning habitat, and mortality at sea. Many of these tangibles we have no control over. We are still able as responsible fishermen to increase opportunities for a growing population and preserve dwindling wild stocks. How? That answer is to practice and promote catch and release steelheading.

I would like to share with you some information from journal records that proves without question that releasing steelhead, especially wild steelhead, will increase opportunities for hookups. I have kept an 11-year record on one tiny Olympic Peninsula river that is virtually isolated from other fishermen due to extremely difficult access. So, to say the least, this was an ideal situation to study the effects of killing steelhead versus releasing them.

The fish that were studied are wild summer-run steelhead that navigate the canyons in the upper stretches of the river. The river here has a series of high waterfalls and deep pools, where the fish must slow down and rest. Thousands of years of natural selection have bred a strain of fish that can leap all these 10- to 15-foot falls with ease. Once hooked, they will commonly jump seven feet in the air! They are truly amazing fish that were almost wiped out because of outdated game laws and fishermen's greed.

Breathtaking, beautiful canyon holes, like this one is where the author's study on releasing native summer steelhead took place.

Four of my fishing partners and myself found and started fishing for these truly unique steelhead in the summer of 1979. I reluctantly admit that when we started fishing here, with very few exceptions every fish landed was killed. No laws were being broken, and we were ignorant of the importance of releasing wild steelhead. There are a few hatchery fish showing every summer, but they are strays because the Washington Dept. of Wildlife does not plant summer steelhead there. It is estimated that the entire run of native summer steelhead in this river is no more than 100 fish. You can see why taking 30 or so fish a year out of the run would be devastating. This was exactly what was happening. A look at the 11-year chart graphically explains this.

We experienced great steelheading for the first three years. Then the numbers started to decrease alarmingly. We first blamed the steelhead shortage on the exploding seal population off the river mouth, which undoubtedly accounted for the loss of some fish, but we were not helping matters by killing every fish landed. Dead steelhead can't spawn. So we all made a pact in 1983 to release every native summer run we landed in the canyon.

The years 1984 and 1985 showed dismal returns, but still each native was diligently put back into the river, usually after a quick photo. All steelhead were fully revived and swam strongly back to their holding water. The only fish kept then and today is the odd hatchery steelhead, with definite clipped, healed-over adipose fins and deformed dorsals. In 1988, '89, and '90, wonderful things started to happen. Instead of making three trips to the canyon to hook one fish, we were hooking one to three steelhead every trip. It had been the best fishing in nine summers.

Our increased success could be due to better water conditions in the spring for increased smolt survival, less mortality at sea or any number of unknown factors. But I firmly believe it's due to the release of all native steelhead which allowed for maximum spawning. The chart shows proof positive. You can see where success per trip had leaped for the better shortly after the decision was made to release wild fish.

I hope this shows the importance of catch and release. Not only does it give another angler a chance to play a fish, it helps protect and preserve precious wild steelhead stocks. If you want to preserve the moment, carry a camera. A picture will capture the fish forever. This method of capture is a great deal more satisfying than watching a once beautiful animal turn into a fading, stiffening length of dead flesh.

Remember, it is up to all of us to protect the fragile native steelhead. Any steelhead, wild or hatchery, is a precious, expensive resource.

ELEVEN YEAR TOTALS FOR SUMMER-RUN NATIVE STEELHEAD (MAY-OCTOBER)

Year	1979	1980	1981	1982	1983*	1984	1985	1986	1987	1988	1989	1990
Steelhead Hooked	19	29	25	14	11	17	8	9	22	38	22	17
Steelhead Landed	11	17	20	10	6	11	6	9	14	26	18	13
Steelhead Killed	11	17	19	8	0	2[1]	1[1]	0	0	2[1]	0	0
Steelhead Released	0	0	1	2	6	9	5	9	14	24	18	13
Trips to River[2]	15	42	38	44	46	32	19	22	32	26	16	9

* = First season of catch and release for native steelhead
[1] = Hatchery steelhead (fin-clipped)
[2] = "Trips" are one angler per day on the river

How To Release Steelhead

Play and release fish as rapidly as possible. A steelhead played with a soft hand for a long period may suffer from lactic acid buildup in the muscle tissue or die from exhaustion.

Keep the steelhead in the water as much as possible, a few to six inches of water is an adequate cushion. Out of water a fish's weight is many times what it is in the water. If you want a photo, gently cradle the fish with one hand under the pectoral fins, and firmly grasp the wrist of the tail with the other. Don't allow the fish to flop on the rocks or sand. This may cause internal damage and will remove the fish's protective slime coat.

Keep fingers out the gill plates; ripped gill rakers will cause excessive bleeding. Remove the hook as rapidly and gently as possible with needle-nose pliers or hemostats. If the steelhead is deeply hooked (extremely rare when using spoons) cut the hook with the pliers and leave it in the fish.

After your take a picture hold the steelhead in slow, flowing water facing upstream. Move it back and forth to push fresh, oxygenated water into its gills. When the steelhead revives it will start to struggle and show strength. When it can swim normally let go of the tail wrist and let it swim away.

1) Cradle fish in the slow flowing portion of the drift it was caught in.

2) Move fish gently back and forth to allow oxygen to circulate through the gills.

3) When the fish shows strength and wants to swim, let go of the tail and let it swim away.

Chapter 8

Last Casts

Remembering and Recognition

During the introduction I promised to shy away from anecdotes, but I want to share one short story that sums up steelhead fishing to me. Perhaps to some of you as well.

One afternoon in late January of '89 I was fortunate enough to shake hands with a tinfoil-bright hatchery steelhead from the McMillan Drift on Washington's Puyallup River. While in the process of cleaning my catch two sets of eyes appeared over my shoulder. Half startled, I whipped around to see two barely teenage boys staring agape at my fish.

While we exchanged greetings and the technique that tricked the steelhead into his fatal mistake (a spoon, naturally), I took note of their mismatched outfits. Two five-foot long, beat-up trout rods and bargain table spinning reels. Neither youngster had a tackle vest or boots. I could tell by the longing look in their eyes that they had never caught a steelhead.

Every time I land a steelhead, using spoons or any technique, my respect and appreciation for the species increases a little bit more.

As we talked, I couldn't help but think back to my first attempts at steelheading on the Puyallup with my Mitchell 300 reel and Eagle Claw glass rod. I remembered being in their shoes 23 years ago – it was so damn awkward. I was so young, so eager, with so much to learn about steelhead. I also remembered what Uncle Bob taught me, and how I, like these youths, hung on each word passed on along these same river banks. I thought back to how it felt watching someone else battle a fresh steelhead and how desperately I wanted to feel the power of one.

We talked steelheading for 15 minutes, discussing simple spoon techniques, proper gear and even touched on ethics. I had to go to work, so I cut off the old, mismatched drift rigs they had on and tied a brass Little Cleo to each of their lines. They were very polite, and I sent them off with a good-luck wish. With their new-found knowledge and "magic" lures, they ran back upstream to the mouth of the Carbon River.

I walked back to my Bronco with a feeling that never had surfaced before. Not from scoring a bright hatchery fish for the barbecue, but from knowing that I had come a full circle as a steelheader. It finally hit me – all the years of learning and all the trial and error put in to reach this level. Passing on a bit of that knowledge to those two young steelheaders, the future of our sport, was extremely satisfying. I thought back to how exciting it was for me to learning new techniques, finally hook and play a fish, and travel and discover new rivers. All veteran steelheaders can relate to this.

When I first met the two teenagers, I really felt sorry for them. An hour later, while driving home, pity changed to jealousy. I wanted to be 14 again – to feel awkward, to be proud of my drugstore rod and reel, to take the first steps down the road to becoming a steelheader. I wanted to solve the mysteries of rivers all over again.

That day on the Puyallup has made me appreciate every minute I get to go fishing. Even when I get skunked (more often than I care to admit in print), I still drink in everything nature has to offer, enjoy the company of my partners, and savor the time spent walking the river banks.

I'm sure that as long as I fish for steelhead, I'll never learn all there is to know about this regal, silvery ghost. I do know, however, that you can love something completely without completely understanding it.